SECOND EDITION
Student's Book
4

SUPER MINDS

Herbert Puchta · Peter Lewis-Jones · Günter Gerngross

CAMBRIDGE
UNIVERSITY PRESS

Map of the book

Well done, Ben and Lucy! (pages 4–9)

Vocabulary	Language focus	Story
At town events	• Present simple questions • Past simple questions	*The map* **Phonics** Rhyming words

▶ Song: The Explorers

1 In the museum (pages 10–21)

How can we learn about the past?

Vocabulary	Language focus	Story	Skills	Think and learn
Knights and queens	• *Must / Mustn't* • Direct and indirect objects	*The knight* **Phonics** The letter sound *ow*	• Reading • Listening and speaking **Value** Learning about your family	History: Timelines

▶ Song: The museum trip ▶ Communication: Living in a museum ▶ Writing: A museum advert

2 The world around us (pages 22–33)

What do we know about the outside world?

Vocabulary	Language focus	Story	Skills	Think and learn
The countryside	• Past simple revision; connectors • *Could / Couldn't*	*At the restaurant* **Value** Making time for the family **Phonics** Silent consonants	• Reading • Listening and writing	Geography: Maps and satellites

▶ Song: The world outside ▶ Communication: What we do in our free time ▶ Writing: My favourite outdoor place

3 Danger! (pages 34–45)

How can water be dangerous?

Vocabulary	Language focus	Story	Skills	Think and learn
Emergencies	• Past continuous • Past continuous questions	*The man in the car* **Phonics** The sound /aɪ/	• Reading • Reading and listening **Value** Learning from nature	Environmental studies: Floods

▶ Song: In the water ▶ Communication: Emergency! ▶ Writing: Story telling

4 Two return tickets (pages 46–57)

What's the best way to travel?

Vocabulary	Language focus	Story	Skills	Think and learn
At the train station	• *at / in / on* • Past continuous and past simple	*The tunnel* **Value** Look after your things carefully **Phonics** The sound /eə/	• Reading • Listening and speaking	Geography: Ways to travel

▶ Song: The fantasy train ▶ Communication: At the train station ▶ Writing: A notice for a school trip

5 Police! (pages 58–69)

How can we describe people?

Vocabulary	Language focus	Story	Skills	Think and learn
Hair and face	• *Used to* • *Had to*	*The Mysterious H* **Phonics** The sounds /ɑː/ and /ɔː/	• Reading • Writing and listening **Value** Mending your ways	Art: Sketches

▶ Song: Who are you? ▶ Communication: Reading habits ▶ Writing: A book review

6 Mythical beasts (pages 70–81)

What were animals like long ago?

Vocabulary	Language focus	Story	Skills	Think and learn
Animal bodies	• Comparatives and superlatives • *It looks like …*	*The secret door* **Value** Always think about safety **Phonics** The letter sound *ea*	• Listening • Speaking and writing	Science: Dinosaurs

▶ Song: My dinosaur book ▶ Communication: Finding an unusual animal ▶ Writing: My beast

7 Orchestra practice (pages 82–93)

How are musical instruments different?

Vocabulary	Language focus	Story	Skills	Think and learn
Musical instruments	• Possessive pronouns • *who / which / where*	*At the concert hall* **Phonics** The sounds /ɜː/ and /ɔː/	• Reading • Writing and listening **Value** Teamwork	Music: Instrument families

▶ Song: The best band in the land ▶ Communication: Music in our class ▶ Writing: My music review

8 In the planetarium (pages 94–105)

Why is space exciting?

Vocabulary	Language focus	Story	Skills	Think and learn
Space	• *Will* • Adverbs	*The trap* **Value** Respecting your elders **Phonics** Word stress and the sound /ə/	• Listening and reading • Speaking and writing	Science: Space

▶ Song: Outer space ▶ Communication: Interview an alien ▶ Writing: A diary entry

9 At the campsite (pages 106–117)

What do we know about camping?

Vocabulary	Language focus	Story	Skills	Think and learn
Holiday activities	• *a bottle / can / loaf / packet / piece of* and *some* • *How much … ? / How many … ?*	*The last line* **Phonics** Unstressed words	• Reading • Reading, listening and speaking **Value** Preparing carefully	Maths: Measurements

▶ Song: I'll make lunch for you ▶ Communication: Holiday plans ▶ Writing: A holiday leaflet

• **Language focus:** pages 118–127

Practice of creative thinking, critical thinking and cognitive skills

Well done, Ben and Lucy!

1 001 Listen and say the words. Then check with a friend.

1 big wheel
2 roller coaster
3 roundabout
4 dodgem cars
5 band
6 mayor
7 microphone
8 journalist
9 photographer

2 002 **Listen and answer.**

1 Where are Ben and Lucy?
2 Why are they there?
3 Who wants to talk to Ben and Lucy?
4 What does Lucy want to do first?

3 **Play the secret word game.**

My secret word is a fairground ride.

Roundabout!

You speak into my secret word.

Microphone!

1 003 Listen and circle.

1	Do you like going on adventures?	a Yes, I love it.	b No, I hate it.
2	Do you want to be famous?	a Yes, I do.	b No, I don't.
3	What do you want to be when you're older?	a An explorer.	b A librarian.
4	What do you like doing in your free time?	a Playing computer games.	b Reading books.
5	Is Lucy your best friend?	a Yes, she is.	b No, she isn't.
6	Does Lucy like Buster?	a Yes, she does.	b No, she doesn't.

2 Put the words in order. Say the sentences.

1 you reading like books? Do

2 next? you want read What do to

3 Ben want to famous? be Does

4 friend? your Is best Ben

3 004 Watch, listen and say.

Language focus

Do you **like** going to the gecko school? Where **do** you **live**? **Is** your life exciting?

Does your brother Greg **like** climbing things? What **do** you **like**? **Are** you famous?

4 Interview a friend. Find out four new things.

Do you want to be famous?

What colour are the walls in your room?

What time do you … ?

What's your favourite … ?

1 005 Listen and tick ✓. Then sing the song.

The Explorers.
Here they come.
Lucy and Ben. Adventure and fun.
The Explorers.
Here they are.
Ben and Lucy. Action stars.

Does Ben like adventure?
Yes, he does.
He loves exploring things,
Just like us.

The Explorers …

Is Lucy scared of anything?
No, she's not.
Does she find much treasure?
Yes, a lot.

The Explorers …

Do they like excitement?
Yes, they do.
Here's their next adventure.
You can join in too!

The Explorers …

Ben	Lucy	
		likes adventure.
		likes exploring.
		isn't scared of anything.
		finds lots of treasure.
		like excitement.

2 What do you like or love doing? Tell a friend.

I like having fun with my friends.

I love walking in the mountains.

1 007 Complete the interview. Listen and check.

school clues castle door statue librarian

Journalist: So, Lucy, tell me about your adventure. How did you find the (1) __________?

Lucy: It all started when we found an old book in the castle.

Journalist: What was in the book?

Lucy: It had a secret code. We needed to break the code and then we used it to read the clues.

Journalist: What did the (2) __________ do?

Lucy: They helped us to find letters.

Journalist: And what did the letters do?

Lucy: We used the letters to make a word. With this word we opened a (3) __________ in the (4) __________ and found the treasure.

Journalist: Was it dangerous?

Lucy: Yes, it was. There were two 'baddies': a man called Horax and a woman called Zelda.

Journalist: Did they want the book?

Lucy: Yes, they wanted the book to find the treasure. They wanted to keep it and we found out later that Horax was our school (5) __________, Mr Williams. We were shocked.

Journalist: Oh, no! Does he still work at your (6) __________?

Lucy: No, he doesn't. We don't know where he is now.

2 Where do the words go? Say the sentences.

what did was did were

1 it dangerous?
2 was in the book?
3 you scared?
4 How you find the statue?
5 they want the book?

3 008 Watch, listen and say.

Language focus

Did you **have** a lot of fun?
How **did** you **get** there?
Was that dangerous?
Were you happy, my dear brother?
What **was** there?

4 Play the guessing game.

Guess what I did in the holidays.

Did you do a lot of sports?

No, I didn't.

Did you go to the beach a lot?

1 009 Where can you see the diamond symbol?

Mr Davidson: Mmm, it really is a beautiful statue. It's very, very old.
Lucy: We had an amazing adventure to find it.
Ben: It was exciting and quite dangerous too.

Mr Davidson: This symbol here ... I know this ...
Lucy: What is it?
Mr Davidson: That's it! Now I remember. Wait here a moment.

Ben: Very strange. What does he remember?
Lucy: And where did he go? Into the museum?
Ben: I think so. But what's that symbol?

Mr Davidson: Here you are. Look at this.
Lucy: What is it?
Mr Davidson: A map from the museum.

Mr Davidson: Look closely. What can you see?

Ben: The symbol! It's the same as on the statue.
Mr Davidson: This diamond is the symbol of an old English king. With this map you can find more of the king's treasure.

Horax: Zelda, it's me. The kids have got a treasure map.
Zelda: We have to follow them and find the treasure before they do.

2 **Answer the questions.**

1 What does Mr Davidson find on the statue? ______

2 Where does he go? ______

3 What does he get? ______

4 What do Ben and Lucy have to make to find the treasure? ______

5 Who is watching them? ______

6 What are Horax and Zelda going to do? ______

Phonics

3 **Find the train and the plane in the story.**

4 010 **Listen and say.**

The boys can make noise, but Sue can too!

1 In the museum

1 Listen and say the words. Then check with a friend. (011)

1 sword
2 bow and arrow
3 helmet
4 crown
5 necklace
6 belt
7 bracelet
8 shield
9 knight
10 queen

BIG QUESTION How can we learn about the past?

2 (012) Listen and correct the sentences.

1 There is a helmet on the map.
2 Ben is talking about the helmet.
3 Lucy would like the queen's crown.
4 They go to the dinosaur room.

3 Ask and answer.

Where's the sword?
The knight's carrying it.
Where's the bracelet?
The queen's wearing it.

1 013 Listen and number the pictures.

2 Complete with *must* or *mustn't*. Say the sentences.

1 I ________ buy a ticket.

2 I ________ speak quietly.

3 I ________ run.

4 I ________ take photos.

3 014 Watch, listen and say.

Language focus

I **must leave** now.
I **mustn't be late**.
I **must hurry**.
Gina doesn't want to wait.

I **must walk** fast.
I **mustn't slow down**.
I **must get**
To the other side of town.

4 Play the *Mustn't forget* game.

1 (015) Listen and tick ☑ the things the girl mustn't touch or use. Then sing the song.

There's a museum trip tomorrow
To learn our history,
But now I'm thinking about the things
My teacher said to me.

I mustn't touch the arrows.
I mustn't touch the bows.
I mustn't touch the swords.
There are so many things
to know!

I must listen quietly
To what my teachers say.
I must write 500 words
About the school trip day.

I mustn't take photos.
I mustn't shout or run.
I mustn't use my mobile phone.
I hope it will be fun!

There's a museum trip tomorrow.
It's going to be fun.
I'm going to be a good girl.
We're going to have fun! [x2]

2 Complete the rules for your History lesson.

1 You must ... 2 You must ... 3 You mustn't ... 4 You mustn't ...

3 Compare your rules with a partner.

In my History lesson you must do your homework.

In my History lesson you mustn't be late.

1 017 Complete the sentences. Listen and check.

necklace coats crown swords shield

1 Give us the ____________, please.

2 Give him the ____________, please.

3 Give me the ____________, please.

4 Give her the ____________, please.

5 Give them the ____________, please.

2 Where do the words go? Say the sentences.

1 Give the cameras, please. (us)

2 Give the pencils, please. (me)

3 Give the apple, please. (her)

4 Give the sandwiches, please. (them)

3 018 Watch, listen and say.

Language focus

Give **him a fly**. Give **them a fly**. Give **me a fly**.

Give **her a fly**. Give **us a fly**.

4 Play the *Show me* game.

Show me the necklace.

The knight

1 019 What do Ben and Lucy see on the shield?

1

Lucy: Now, let's look for the first line of the rhyme.
Ben: I really hope we can find it here.

2

Ben: Help! That was close!
Lucy: Where did it come from?
Ben: I don't know, but someone is trying to hurt us.

3

Ben: I can't see anyone.
Lucy: Look, there's a knight with a sword. He's coming after us. Let's run.

4

Ben: Look, this is a good place to hide.
Lucy: I hope the knight doesn't find us.
Ben: Shhh. We mustn't make a noise.

5

Lucy: I've got an idea. Hold the lead. Buster, come here!
Ben: That's it, Buster! Good dog!

6

Ben: That was a brilliant idea.
Lucy: I'm glad it worked. I was very scared.

7

Ben: Look! The knight's shield! It's the first symbol! And there's the line of the rhyme.

Lucy: Let me see. 'Behind the picture in the frame.' We must write it down.

8

Zelda: Poor Horax. How do you feel?

Horax: Terrible! I'm going to get those children.

Zelda: And their map.

2 Answer the questions.

Who …

1 sees the knight first? ________

2 finds a place to hide? ________

3 is on a lead? ________

4 has a brilliant idea? ________

5 sees the shield? ________

6 doesn't feel very well? ________

Phonics

3 Find the crown and the arrow in the story.

4 020 Listen and say.

Now give me the bow, crown and arrow from the window, please.

1 **Look at the pictures in Activity 2. Answer the questions.**

Where can you see …

1 a woman drinking tea and pulling a face?

2 a girl looking at some sweets?

3 a baby with a green face?

4 a dog that can't swim?

2 021 **Read and listen. Match the pictures with the stories.**

Family Stories

Family stories are important. They help us learn about who we are and where we come from. Every family has a story teller. My Aunt Jill tells lots of great stories about when she was a child. She often talks about my dad (her younger brother), my grandfather and grandmother (her mum and dad), and their dog. Here are four of my favourites.

a

b

c

d

1 One day, the family went for a walk by the river with their dog. The dog saw some birds near the river. He wanted to get the birds, so he pulled on the lead and my grandpa dropped it. The dog ran. The birds saw him and flew away. The dog tried to stop but he couldn't, so he fell into the river. But he wasn't good at swimming! Grandpa jumped into the water and helped him to get out.

2 When my dad was a baby he always wore green clothes. Green was my grandmother's favourite colour. But Aunt Jill didn't like my dad because everybody wanted to see him, so they forgot about her. Jill liked painting – she painted all day, every day. One day, when her mother was in the kitchen, Jill looked at her baby brother and had a great idea. When her mother came back from the kitchen she almost dropped her cup of tea. Her baby had a green face and he was laughing!

3 One day, when Aunt Jill was about seven, her mother had some friends at the house for a cup of tea. Jill wanted to help, so her mother asked her to get the sugar. Jill went into the kitchen, got the sugar bowl and put it on the table. One of her mother's friends put some sugar in her tea. A few minutes later when the lady drank her tea she pulled a horrible face. The sugar wasn't sugar – it was salt! 'I'm very sorry, I got the wrong bowl from the kitchen,' said Jill sadly.

4 One day, when my aunt was about four, she went shopping with her dad – my grandpa. He is famous in the family because he always forgets things. He got the bread and walked out of the shop. Jill was busy. She was looking at the sweets and didn't see her dad leave. Grandpa was almost home when he remembered Jill. He ran back to the shop, terrified. Jill was still by the sweets. 'Jill,' he said. 'I'm so sorry I forgot you. Are you OK?' Jill looked up happily and said, 'I'm fine. Can I have these sweets, please?'

3 **Which stories do these last lines come from?**

a Her mother wasn't very happy. __

b Luckily, all the women thought it was really funny. __

c When he got out he was very wet. __

d 'Of course you can!' her dad said. __

4 **What do you think of each story? Compare with a friend.**

😃 = I love it. 😐 = It's OK. 😞 = I don't like it.

5 022 **Listen to another story and answer the questions.**

1 How old was Jill in the story?

2 Where was the family on holiday?

3 Why didn't Jill's dad use sun cream?

4 What was her dad's face like when he woke up?

5 What does Jill's dad always do now?

TIMELINES

Watch and answer. How do timelines help us learn about the past?

1 Listen and point. 023

1 **900** nine hundred

2 **1200** twelve hundred

3 **1550** fifteen fifty

4 **1825** eighteen twenty-five

5 **1960** nineteen sixty

6 **2007** two thousand and seven

7 **2014** twenty fourteen

2 Look, read and write the years in the timeline.

1350 1520 2010 600

1 around ________
This very old helmet was made for a king. People found it in 1939 on a boat under the ground.

3 around ________
A king wore this necklace to show that he had a lot of money.

500 1000 1500 2000

2 around ________
This beautiful crown was made for a German queen.

4 ________
This is the ring of the famou princess, Kate Middleton.

3 Look at the timeline again. Answer the questions.

1 What was made around 1520? ________

2 What is the oldest thing on the timeline? ________

3 What is the newest thing on the timeline? ________

4 Which things are newer than the helmet? ________

5 Which things are older than the necklace? ________

4 Look at the timeline. What year do you think these helmets are from? Draw lines.

Super fact!
The first bicycle helmet was made in 1975.

Timeline of modern helmets

a

b

c

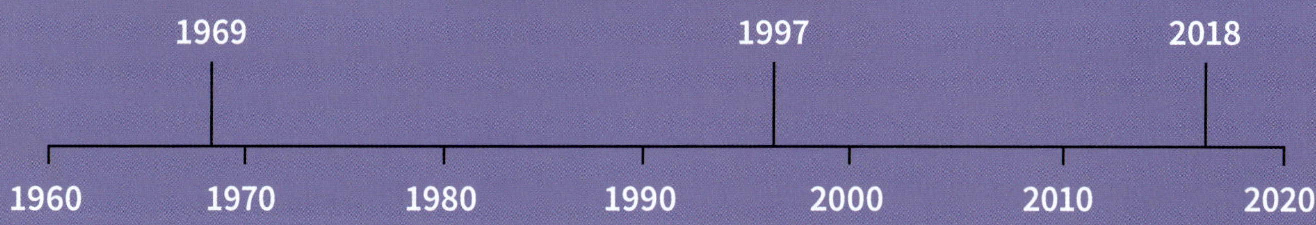

5 024 Now listen and check.

6 Project Think of four things in your house. How old are they? Make a timeline for them.

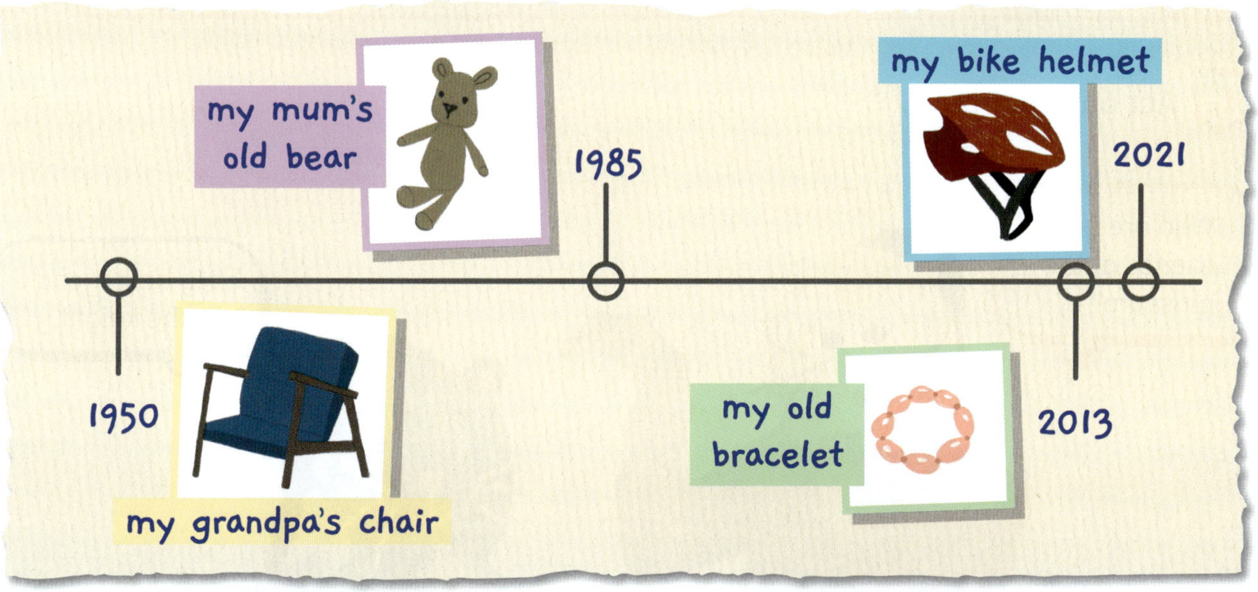

Talk and find out

Living in a museum

1 Choose a role card. Read and plan.

Student A

You are a cat who lives in a museum. One night another cat comes to see you at the museum. Talk to him / her about:

- your friends at the museum
- what you do in the museum in the day
- what you do at night
- your favourite exhibits

Student B

You are a cat living near the museum. One night you go to visit your friend at the museum. Ask him / her questions about life there. You'd like to know about:

- the cat's friends at the museum
- what the cat does during the day
- what the cat does at night
- the cat's favourite exhibits

Useful language

Cat friend
Who are your friends at the museum?
What do you do … ?
Show me your favourite exhibit.
What is it?

Museum cat
My best friends are …
In the day I … / At night I …
My favourite exhibit …

2 Act out your play.

A museum advert

1 Start a new portfolio for this year. Write your profile.

My name:
My class:
My teacher's name:
People in my family:

My favourite sport:
My favourite music:
My favourite food and drink:

2 You are going to make an advert. Visit a museum or find out about it on the internet. Make notes.

Name of museum: Museum in the Park
What you can learn: history of Woodville
Exhibits: old photos, ancient jewellery
Opening hours: Mon–Fri 9 am–4 pm
Other facts: café, shop (books, key rings, postcards, posters)

3 Read the advert. What makes it boring? How could you make it better?

Come to WOODVILLE and visit our INTERESTING MUSEUM

It's called the Museum in the Park. Come here to learn interesting things about the history of our town. There are lots of interesting photos in the museum. They show life in our town a long time ago. The most important exhibit is an interesting collection of ancient jewellery. The Museum in the Park is open from 9 am to 4 pm. There is also a nice café and a shop where you can buy interesting books, key rings, postcards and posters.

Writing tip

Use adjectives to help make your writing more interesting.

4 Make your advert. How many adjectives are there in it?

2 The world around us

1 Listen and say the words. Then check with a friend. (025)

1 mountain
2 forest
3 village
4 field
5 lake
6 island
7 river
8 path

BIG QUESTION What do we know about the outside world?

2 (026) Listen and answer.

1 Why isn't Ben ready to walk?
2 Why is Buster barking?
3 Where are they going next?
4 How long will it take?

3 Play *I spy*.

I spy, with my little eye, something with a 't' in it.

Is it 'path'?

1 027 Listen, read and answer the questions.

Last Sunday, the weather was sunny, so we went for a walk. We took a picnic in a basket. We walked through the forest and arrived at a lake. In the middle of the lake there was a small island. There was a long, thin bridge, so we walked over it to the island. We liked the island because there were beautiful flowers there. We wanted to have a picnic, but our basket fell into the lake!

1 What did Alice walk through?

____

2 What was in the middle of the lake?

____

3 How did they get to the island?

____

4 What fell into the water?

____

2 Put the words in order. Say the sentences.

1 We went for a walk last Sunday … weather sunny. the was because

2 We walked over the bridge … and we island. arrived the at

3 There were lots of beautiful flowers … the liked so island. we

4 We wanted to eat, … our the but fell water. basket into

3 028 Watch, listen and say.

Language focus

We climbed a tree, **but** it was too high.

We wanted to have fun, **so** we climbed a tower.

We got to the top **and** we saw a bee.

Then we climbed down again **because** bees scare me!

4 Make sentences with *because*, *so*, and or *but*.

I watched a film …

I didn't meet my friends …

We didn't play volleyball …

I went to bed early …

I went to bed early and I read a book.

I went to bed early because …

1 029 Listen and number the pictures. Then sing the song.

Take a look at the world outside
And all the things there are to do,
To see, to smell, to taste, to touch!
Let's go out there, me and you.

We swam in the river
Because it was so hot.
We climbed up the mountain
And reached the top.

Take a look at the world outside ...

We walked through the forest,
The forest near our town.
We played in the fields
And watched the sun go down.

Take a look at the world outside ...

We fished in a little lake.
But we didn't catch a thing,
So we built a boat from wood
And sailed around like kings.

Take a look at the world outside ...

2 List activities you can do in these places. Which place would you like to visit more?

3 Share your ideas with a friend.

I'd like to visit the island because we can camp, swim and have a picnic.

1 031 Listen and number the pictures.

2 Complete with *could*. Say the sentences.

1 I swim for ten hours!

2 I jump higher than a tree!

3 032 Watch, listen and say.

Language focus

Tell me, Gina, all about you.
When you were young, what **could** you **do**?
Could you **read**? **Could** you **write**?
Could you **jump** down from a big height?

When I was young, ten years ago,
I **couldn't read** and I **couldn't write**.
But I **could catch** the fastest flies
And I **could** always **see** at night.

4 Tell stories about yourself, the Super Baby.

1 033 What does Grandpa put in Ben's pocket?

1

Lucy: What a nice restaurant!

Ben: Look at our treasure map, Grandpa.

Grandpa: Oh, yes! Ah, but here's our soup. Let's look at the map after lunch.

2

Grandpa: So, it's a treasure map. What are you looking for?

Lucy: There are pictures on the map. We have to find these pictures and the lines of a rhyme.

3

Waiter: Here's your bread.

Lucy: The next picture on the map is a lion. Maybe the next line is at the zoo.

Ben: But you don't find red lions at the zoo!

4

Ben: Oh, no! The map!

Lucy: What is it?

Ben: It isn't in my pocket and it isn't on the floor.

5

Grandpa: Ben, Lucy ... did you want this?

Ben: But where ... how did you get that?

Grandpa: You must be more careful!

6

Grandpa: There was something strange about that waiter. I put a menu in your pocket and kept the map. The waiter took the menu.

 Value: making time for the family; reading for pleasure

7

Grandpa: Hmm, that waiter looked like a man that I knew a long time ago. I can tell you later, but first I want to talk about this picture of the red lion.

8

Lucy: The Red Lion! It's this restaurant!
Grandpa: Yes, and now look at the menu.
Ben: It's the symbol and the line! It says: 'Lots of stairs. Climb thirty-three!'

2 Put the story in order.

- ☐ Ben and Lucy show the map to Grandpa.
- ☐ Grandpa asks the children about the map.
- ☐ Grandpa shows Ben and Lucy the menu.
- ☐ The waiter brings the bread.
- ☐ Grandpa helps them to find the line.
- ☐ Ben can't find the map.

Phonics

3 Find the swords in the story.

4 034 Listen and say.

A rhino writing a rescue sign on an island.

1 Read the story. Choose a word from the box. Write the correct word next to numbers 1–6. There are four extra pictures.

apple

banana

bus

car

hour

house

river

forest

restaurant

minute

Last month my parents and I went for a walk. First we drove for an hour and then we parked the **(1)** __________. Next we walked through a **(2)** __________ and saw nothing but trees for two hours. Then we walked another hour to the top of a mountain. We sat down and looked around. Then Mum said to Dad, 'Can you give me a sandwich and an **(3)** __________?' Dad put his hand in the rucksack and looked sad. Mum and I looked at Dad. He couldn't find any sandwiches. 'I'm sorry,' he said, 'I think they're on the table in the kitchen.' Mum and I weren't happy.

We were very hungry. 'I've got an idea,' Dad said. 'We'll go down a different way, to the lake. Near the lake there's a village and there's a good restaurant there.' We stood up and started to go down. When we came to a small **(4)** __________, we had to take off our shoes and socks to get to the other side. After two hours, we got to the lake and then we saw the village. We walked over, but there wasn't a **(5)** __________ in the village. 'Where is our car, Dad?' I asked. 'Well, I think it's only an **(6)** __________ away,' he answered.

2 Now choose the best name for the story.

☐ A mountain walk ☐ A day without food ☐ The village without a restaurant

1 035 **What did James do last week? Look at the pictures. Then listen and draw lines.**

a

b

Monday

Tuesday

Wednesday

Thursday

Friday

c

d

e

2 036 **Listen again and write *yes* or *no*.**

1 Monday was a rainy day. ________

2 James and his grandpa had a picnic in the countryside. ________

3 James's sister is getting a bike for her birthday. ________

4 On Thursday, James bought some butter. ________

5 James's best friend is Rick. ________

3 **Write about the outdoor activities you did last week.**

On Monday I rode my bike with my best friend, Tom. We went to a little village. On Tuesday I visited my grandpa and we played football in his garden. He lives in the city. I went there by bus.

Maps and satellites

Watch and answer. How can we learn about places?

Super fact!

We can use satellite images to tell us what the weather is going to be like.

1 Listen and point. 037

satellite

satellite image

continent

country

city

city centre

2 Read about maps and satellite images. Then tick ☑.

Maps and satellite images help us to learn about places around the world. They use different technology.

Maps are pictures that show places and some of the things in them. They can help people to find places in cities, like streets and hospitals. Some maps show continents and some show city centres. Some maps only show one kind of place, like mountains or rivers.

Satellite images are photos of places. Satellites take these photos from space. The images show everything that is in these places at the time the satellite takes the photo. Satellite images can show how places are different at different times of year.

	Maps	Satellite images
They help people find places in towns.		
They show how places change.		
They show everything in a place.		
They show only some of the things in the place.		

3 Look at the map and satellite image of the same city. What differences can you see?

This is the café.

4 Point to the places in the satellite image and tell your friend.

hospital airport café cinema bus station school playground

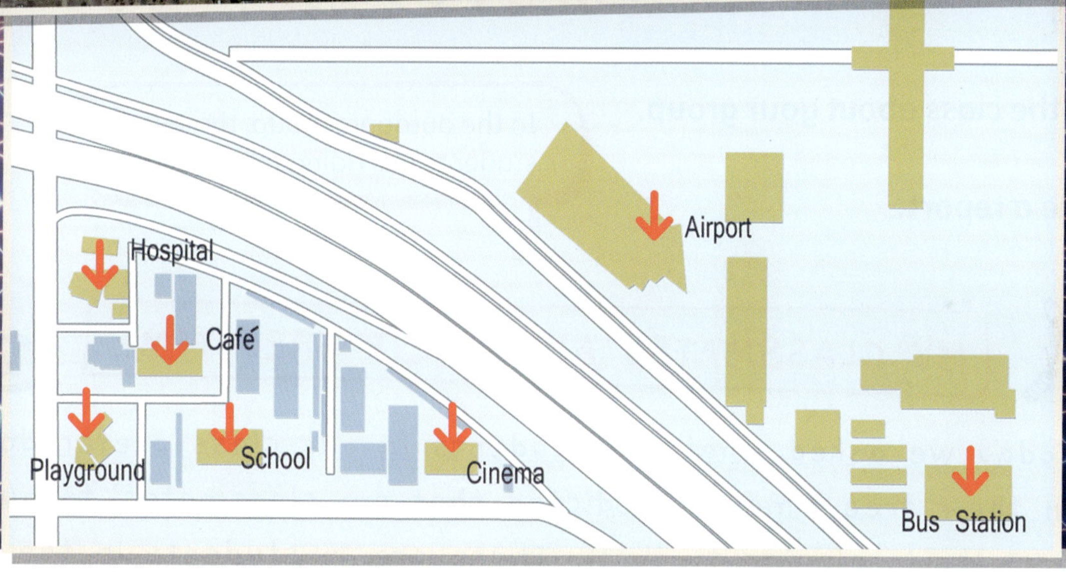

5 Project Find a map or a satellite image of where you live and label your five favourite places. Tell your friends.

My favourite places are my house, the library, the swimming pool, the park and Dan's house.

Talk and find out

What we do in our free time

1 **Make a prediction.**

I predict that my classmates' favourite free time activity is ______________________.

2 **Work in three groups: 'outdoors', 'in town' and 'at home'. Ask about favourite activities. Make a chart.**

What do you like to do outdoors?

What do you like to do in town?

What do you like to do at home?

Outdoors	In town	At home
ride bike ✓✓✓	museum ✓	computer ✓✓
walk ✓	shopping ✓✓	TV ✓

3 **Tell the class about your group.**

In the outdoors group, three students like riding their bike …

4 **Write a report.**

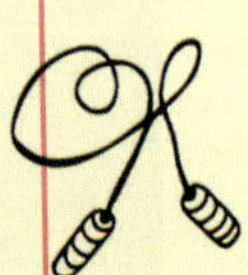

MY CLASSMATES AND THEIR FREE TIME

Today we asked what the students in our class prefer doing in their free time. I predicted that my classmates' favourite activity is playing football. There are 16 students in the class. Half of them (8 students) say that they love being outdoors in their free time. They love riding their bikes (2), going for walks (5) and playing football (1). 5 students (4 girls and 1 boy) prefer spending their free time in town. They love going to museums, shopping and going to the cinema. So now I know that my classmates' favourite free time activity isn't playing football, it's going for walks.

My favourite outdoor place

1 Read Joshua's description and answer the questions.

My favourite outdoor place is my grandma's garden. I like it because there are lots of trees and flowers. It's a very quiet garden. I often sit under my favourite apple tree and listen to the birds. My little sister likes the garden too but she's very noisy, so the birds fly away.

1 Where is Joshua's favourite outdoor place?
2 Why does he like it so much?
3 What does he do when he sits under his favourite tree?
4 Why is his little sister a problem in the garden?

2 Underline *and*, *because*, *but* and *so* in Joshua's text.

3 Join the sentences. so | because | but | and

1 I like the park very much ... on Sundays there are too many people there.
2 On Sundays, my mum and I often go to the forest ... we have a picnic.
3 My best friend lives near a lake ... I go swimming with his family in the summer.
4 I like the river ... I love watching the fish in it.

4 Write about your favourite outdoor place. Use *and*, *because*, *but* and *so*.

- Where's your favourite outdoor place?
- Why do you like it?
- What do you like so much about it?
- What do you do there?

Writing tip

Try to make longer sentences using words like *and*, *but*, *so* and *because*.

3 Danger!

1 Listen and say the words. Then check with a friend. 038

1. fire
2. flood
3. emergency services
4. police car
5. police officer
6. fire engine
7. firefighter
8. ambulance
9. paramedic

BIG QUESTION How can water be dangerous?

2 039 Listen and correct the sentences.

1. The children know Grandpa's story.
2. Grandpa has an accident.
3. A woman's car is on fire.
4. Lucy phones the emergency services.

3 Make short dialogues. Use the words from Activity 1.

999. Emergency services. How can I help you?

There's a flood in Green Street. Can you send a boat … ?

1 040 Guess the picture for each sentence. Listen and check.

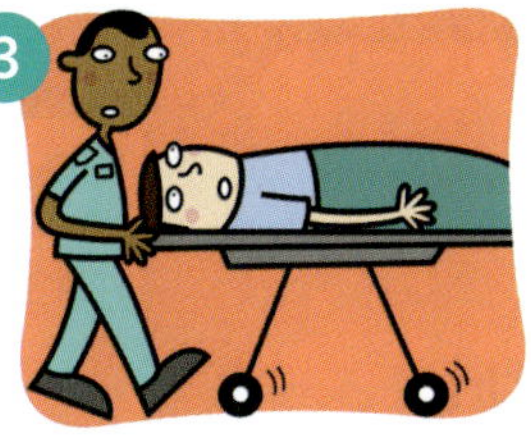

a I was running around with my friends. ☐

b I was playing near the pool and hit my head. ☐

c My friend Sandra and I were climbing a tree. ☐

d My dad and I were riding our bikes and we took him to hospital. ☐

2 Complete with the correct form of the words. Say the sentences.

ride play climb run

Yesterday at 5 o'clock …

1 I ______________ football.

2 I ______________ a tree.

3 My friend and I ______________ our bikes.

4 We ______________ in a race.

3 041 Watch, listen and say.

Language focus

I **was climbing** up a tree.
Gina **was climbing** next to me.
I **was singing** – it was great.
Gina **was singing** – she was great.
We **were singing** a happy song.
But there was something really wrong.

4 Complete the sentences.

When the phone rang,

1 Ella …

2 Jack …

3 Holly …

4 Charlie …

1 042 Listen and number the pictures. Then sing the song.

Look before you jump in,
Jump into the water.
You never know what's waiting,
Waiting in the water.

I was swimming in the sea.
In the sea, I didn't see,
I didn't see the silver shark
Was swimming next to me.

Look before you jump in, ...

I was playing by the lake,
By the lake – my mistake!
I fell in. I didn't see.
But the water wasn't deep.

Look before you jump in, ...

I was running down the street
With new shoes on my feet.
But then I ran straight in
To a flood up to my chin.

Look before you jump in, ...

2 Look at the pictures above. Say what happened to the girl.

First, she was swimming in the sea. But then …

Next, she was playing …

3 Work with a partner. Close your eyes. Imagine what happened to the girl the next day.

She was …

She didn't see …

1 044 Look, read and number the dialogues. Listen and check.

a 'What were you doing yesterday afternoon?' 'I was taking the dog for a walk.' ☐
b 'What was she doing at four?' 'She was reading a book.' ☐
c 'Was he watching TV yesterday evening?' 'Yes, he was.' ☐
d 'Were they playing on a games console?' 'No, they weren't.' ☐

2 Put the words in order. Say the sentences.

1 he 7 o'clock? was What doing at
2 homework you afternoon? your Were yesterday doing

3 045 Watch, listen and say.

Language focus

What **was** he **doing** yesterday at five?
Was he **swimming** in the sea?
No, he **wasn't**!
Was he **watching** TV?
Yes, he **was**.
Were they **playing** yesterday at eight?
No, they **weren't**.
Were they **sleeping** yesterday at eight?
Yes, they **were** – it was late!

4 Ask and answer about yesterday. Find two things you were doing at the same time.

What were you doing at 4 o'clock?

I was doing my homework.
Were you doing your homework?

No, I wasn't. Were you eating dinner at 6 o'clock?

Yes, I was.

Me too!

1 046 Where is Lucy when she makes the phone call?

1

Grandpa: Take the phone, Lucy. I'm going to help that man.

Ben: Can I come with you, Grandpa?

Grandpa: No way. Stay in the car, please.

2

Lucy: My friend's grandpa has got a fire extinguisher and he's going to help the man in the car.

Operator: Good, but *you* mustn't get out, OK?

3

Operator: Now, Mill Road is a long road. Can you see the number on a house from the car?

Lucy: Yes, I can. We're in front of number 92.

4

Operator: All right. Just wait a few more minutes for the ambulance and the fire engine.

Lucy: I think I can hear the ambulance now!

5

Ben: Wow! Look at Grandpa!

Lucy: He's fantastic!

6

Grandpa: Quick! We must get you out.

Man: Agh, my leg!

7

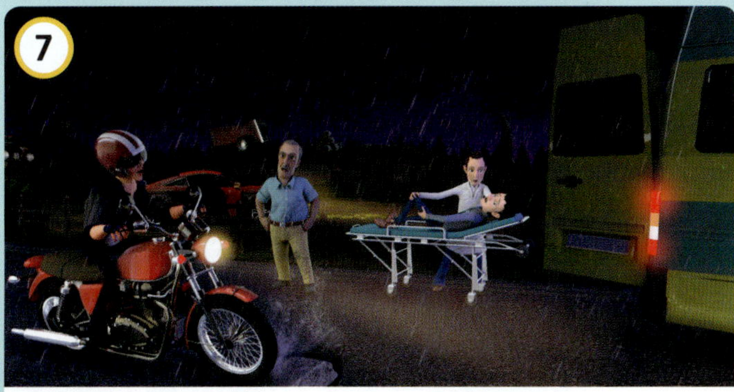

Man: I wasn't driving very fast, but suddenly there was this flood ...

Grandpa: Hey, you on the motorbike! Don't go so fast! *(He thinks)* Hmm. It's him again.

8

Lucy: You were fantastic. You saved the man's life!

Ben: And now tell us the story, Grandpa!

Grandpa: Another time. I'm too tired now.

2 **Read and make sentences.**

1 Ben's grandpa and the children
2 Suddenly, they saw
3 A man was in the car
4 Lucy talked to
5 Grandpa helped the man
6 Grandpa couldn't tell them the story

a and the car was on fire.
b because he was too tired.
c were driving in the rain.
d to get out of the car.
e an accident.
f the emergency services.

Phonics

3 **Find the bike and the lights in the story.**

4 047 **Listen and say.**

Hi, it's not fine. Call my firefighters! There's a fire in Brighton.

1 Look at the pictures in Activity 2. Why do you think the animals are running up the hill?

2 048 Read and listen. Check your answer.

DANGER ON THE BEACH

A long time ago, ten-year-old Aroon and his family were on the beach. Aroon was riding Bejak, their donkey. Bejak was a very friendly donkey. Aroon's dad was getting some wood on the beach, and Aroon was helping him. They wanted to cook a fish for the family. Suddenly Bejak got very nervous. He started to jump around and Aroon fell off the donkey. He landed on the sand. 'Bejak, what's wrong with you? Stop, Bejak, stop!' Aroon shouted. But Bejak was running away – towards the hills.

'That's strange!' Aroon's dad said. Bejak was very important for Aroon's family. He helped them a lot with their work. Aroon's dad called Aroon and his sister, and he called their mum too. 'We have to go and find Bejak,' he said. Aroon, his sister and their mum and dad started to walk. They walked away from the beach, and then they walked up into the hills.

The sun was shining. It was very hot. Aroon and his sister were tired. But they wanted to find Bejak. Then Aroon's dad said, 'Look at these dogs. They are running away from the beach too. And can you see the two elephants over there? That's very strange!' Aroon and his sister stopped. Then they saw the elephants. They were running towards the hills too.

Suddenly Aroon's sister shouted, 'Hey, look at the sea. It's gone!' They all turned round. The sea was a long way out! It looked strange. 'I think there's going to be a tsunami,' Aroon's dad said, and he looked worried. 'A tsunami?' Aroon and his sister asked. 'Yes, it's a very big wave. And it's a terrible thing.'

Suddenly the sea came back towards the beach. It was strong and fast. It broke the houses and the trees near the beach. It killed many people. Aroon and his family were safe, thanks to their donkey, Bejak. They found him near the top of the hill.

The next day Aroon talked to a man from the village. He told him the story about Bejak. The man said, 'Animals know when there is danger from the sea. They always go to higher ground. Your donkey saved your life.'

3 **Put the story in order.**

- [1] One day Aroon and his dad were on the beach.
- [ ] Aroon and his family were safe, thanks to Bejak.
- [ ] Aroon was riding Bejak, their donkey.
- [ ] Aroon fell off.
- [ ] It broke lots of houses and killed many people.
- [ ] Suddenly a very big wave came.
- [ ] Bejak got nervous and started to jump.
- [ ] The family started to look for Bejak.
- [ ] They walked towards the hills.
- [ ] Bejak ran away towards the hills.

4 049 **Listen to a summary of the story. Write the four differences.**

In the summary we have …

1 grass instead of sand.
3 ______ instead of ______.
2 ______ instead of ______.
4 ______ instead of ______.

Floods

Watch and answer. How do floods happen?

snow

ice

1 050 Listen and point.

riverbank

land

wave

melt

flood

2 Read and circle the correct words.

Floods happen when water from a river or the sea goes over the land. They can happen very slowly or very quickly.

Floods often happen when:

- there is a lot of rain.
- snow melts quickly and the water floods the land below.
- a river has too much water in it and the water goes over the riverbanks.
- big waves go over the sea walls onto the land next to the sea.

Floods can be bad for habitats because plants and animals get a lot of water too quickly. But sometimes floods can help plants and animals because they can bring water to very dry habitats.

1 Floods often happen when it's very **sunny** / **rainy** / **windy**.

2 Floods can also happen when snow melts **slowly** / **quietly** / **quickly**.

3 Sometimes a flood can be bad for plants and animals because they get too much **water** / **snow** / **sun**.

4 Sometimes floods can help plants and animals in **dry** / **wet** / **cold** habitats.

3 Look at the pictures. Why are these floods happening?

I think the flood in picture 1 is happening because …

4 Look at the picture and write the letters.

a There's a flood in the village.

b There's a lot of rain.

c There are big waves coming from the sea.

d The snow is melting.

e The water is going over the riverbank.

5 Where is the nearest big river to your school? Write notes.

Name of river	Where does it start?	Where does it meet the sea?	Does it flood? Where? When?

6 Project Write a poem about floods.

- Imagine a flood.
- Where is it? Why is it happening?
- Write ten words that you could use in your poem.
- Write your poem.

Super fact!

Today, people can use computers and satellites to find out when and where a flood is going to happen.

Ice melts,
The river is cold and full.
Over the riverbank,
The water floods the land.
The snow is falling.

Water runs
All over the beach.
Very wet
Everywhere.
Swim!

This poem is an 'acrostic'. Each sentence starts with one letter from the word 'waves'. You can write an acrostic poem if you want to.

Talk and find out

Emergency!

1 Choose a role card. Read and plan.

Student A

Imagine there is an emergency situation. You want to call the emergency services. Before you do, think about the following:

- What is the emergency?
- Where are you?
- Who needs help?
- Who is with you?

Student B

Imagine you work for the emergency services.

- Find out what the problem is.
- Ask where the caller is.
- Find out who needs help.
- Find out who the caller is with.

Useful language

Emergency services	Caller
Hello, this is … How can we help you?	I'm calling because there is a fire / an accident / a flood, …
Where are you calling from?	I'm in … (Street / Road / Lane), opposite / near / in front of the …
Who needs help?	A child / man / woman. He / She can't … He / She is in pain …
Who is with you? Are you safe?	I'm on my own. / There is a … Yes, I am. / No, I'm not because …
OK. Don't worry. The police / an ambulance / a fire engine will be there in …	Thanks very much.

2 Act out your play.

Story telling

1 **Read Amy's stories about the same accident. Underline the words and sentences in Text B that are not in Text A. Which text is better? Why?**

A

It was last May. We were on our bikes. There was some water on the road. My friend Adrian rode into the water. It was deep. He fell.

B

It was a beautiful day last May. 'Let's ride our bikes!' my friends shouted. 'Great!' I said. We had lots of fun. It was sunny and warm. There was some water on the road. 'Watch me!' shouted my friend Adrian. He rode his bike quickly into the water. It was really deep. Suddenly he fell. 'Ouch!' he shouted. Poor Adrian was very wet!

2 **Read Joel's story. Then write it again to make it more interesting.**

It was last weekend. My mum and I wanted to visit my grandparents. We were in the car. We saw an accident. Mum phoned the ambulance. Mum phoned the police. They came ten minutes later.

3 **Now write a story about an accident. It can be a true story or you can imagine it.**

1 Think about the accident in your story.

- When did it happen?
- Who were you with?
- What were you doing?
- What happened?
- Who was hurt?

2 Use some of the underlined words and sentences from Activity 1 and from your version of Joel's story to make it interesting.

3 Draw a picture.

Writing tip

Adding speech to stories makes them more interesting. Remember to use '…'.

4 Two return tickets

1 051 **Listen and say the words. Then check with a friend.**

1 stairs
2 escalator
3 ticket office
4 platform
5 train driver
6 station
7 a cup of coffee
8 a cup of tea
9 rucksack
10 suitcase

BIG QUESTION What's the best way to travel?

2 052 **Listen and answer.**

1 Where do Ben and Lucy decide to go?
2 How much are the tickets?
3 When does their train leave?
4 What do they do before they leave?

3 **Play the prices game.**

Two return tickets to London, please.

OK.

How much is it?

That's £42.

1 🎧 053 Match the questions with the answers. Listen and check.

1 When does the train leave?

2 When are you going to eat next?

3 When's your birthday?

4 When did you get this watch?

5 When are you going to give me my present?

6 When are we going to play football?

a In the afternoon. We're going to meet in the park at three.

b I'm not sure. In 2011, I think.

c At dinner time.

d On your birthday.

e At 8 o'clock from platform 2.

f It's in May.

2 Complete with *in*, *at* or *on*. Say the sentences.

1 My birthday is _________ March.

2 The bus leaves _________ 3 o'clock.

3 Let's go to the cinema _________ Friday.

4 I'm always tired _________ the morning.

5 We sometimes go to Italy _________ the summer.

3 ▶ 🎧 054 Watch, listen and say.

Language focus

In winter **at** nine **at** night
I'm in bed because it's too dark.
In August **at** nine **at** night
I'm still playing in the park!

On Sunday **at** eight **in** the morning
I go out and have a long run.
On Monday **at** six **in** the evening
I meet up with friends for some fun.

4 Play the true or false game.

Number 2 is false.

That's right.

1 I have piano lessons on Tuesdays.

2 I like reading outside in the summer.

3 I go to bed at 10 o'clock.

1 055 Listen and tick ☑ the places you hear. Then sing the song.

The best way to travel is
The fantasy train.
It's leaving at six,
From a platform in your brain.

You don't need a ticket,
This ride is free.
And the drivers of this train,
Are you and me.

A castle on Monday,
The beach in spring,
The town on Sunday,
Let's go and see these things.

The best way to travel is ...

The mountains in the morning,
A country far away,
The stars in the evening,
Let's see this world today.

You don't need a ticket,
This ride is free.
And the drivers of this train,
Are you and me.

The best way to travel is ...

2 Where do you want to visit on the fantasy train? Write a verse for the song.

____________________ ____________________
________________ in spring, Let's go and see these things.

3 Ask and answer.

Where do you want to go on the fantasy train?

I want to go to the Amazon rainforest.

When do you want to go there?

In the summer.

1 Look, read and tick ☑ the correct sentences.

1 When the train arrived, a man was reading a paper. ☐
2 Two girls with rucksacks were waiting on the platform. ☐
3 A man was cleaning the windows of the ticket office. ☐
4 Two dogs were playing with a ball. ☐
5 A boy was eating a pizza and two men were eating hot dogs. ☐

2 Put the words in order. Say the sentences.

1 eating When you was dinner. me I phoned
2 was over. when football fell She playing she

3 057 Watch, listen and say.

Language focus

I **was walking** up the wall, when I **had** a little fall.
When a man **opened** the door, I **was lying** on the floor.

4 Work with a friend. Think of sentences.

1 When I came home from school, our dog …
2 My dad … when I came into the living room.
3 When my parents came home, my big brother and I …
4 When I came into the garden, my friends …
5 My teacher … when I arrived at school.
6 When I started my homework, my sister …

1 058 What happens to Zelda and Horax's tickets?

1

Lucy: I'm still thinking of your grandpa's story. When is he going to tell us?

Ben: I don't know, but I hope it's good!

Lucy: Our train is coming now. Quiet, Buster!

2

Ben: What stop is this?

Lucy: Let's see. It's Broom. ... Oh, no! Horax and Zelda! I hope they can't see us.

Ben: Get away from the window!

3

Horax: Ha! You can't escape! Where's the map?

Lucy: We haven't got it here.

Horax: Open your rucksacks.

4

Horax: Zelda, check the book. Maybe they put the map in there.

Ben: Look! We're going into a tunnel. Now's our chance!

5

Ben: Buster, good dog. Say hello!

Horax: Yuck! Get down! Stop that dog! Zelda, stand near the door! Those kids mustn't escape!

6

Conductor: Tickets, please ... thank you.

Horax: Hey, our tickets! I put them in my hat.

Zelda: Oh, no! Our tickets disappeared when we were going through the tunnel.

 Value: look after your things carefully; reading for pleasure

Conductor: You must get off the train at the next station.
Horax: But I had the tickets.
Conductor: Here's the station now. Off you go.

Lucy: That trick of yours was great. Look at Horax and Zelda. They don't look very happy!
Ben: Lucy, look over there! I don't believe it. It's the line: 'Climb more stairs and look out west'.

2 Put the story in order.

- ☐ Horax and Zelda have to get off the train.
- ☐ In the tunnel Lucy takes Horax and Zelda's tickets.
- ☐ Ben sees the line of the rhyme.
- ☐ At Broom station Lucy sees Horax and Zelda.
- ☐ Lucy and Ben get on the train.
- ☐ The conductor wants to see the tickets.
- ☐ Horax looks for the map in Ben's rucksack.
- ☐ Horax can't find their tickets.

Phonics

3 Find the stairs and the pear in the story.

4 059 Listen and say.

Take care! There's a bear on the stairs at the airport.

1 Read the story. Write some words to complete the sentences about the story. You can use 1, 2 or 3 words.

'Look at the sun,' said Mum. 'Let's go to the beach.'

'Good idea,' I said. But Dad wasn't happy.

'I don't want to drive,' he said. 'The roads will be busy.'

'Don't worry,' said Mum. 'We can take the train.'

Dad looked on his tablet. 'That's a good idea. There's a train at 10 o'clock. Platform 3. Let's hurry.'

'Can I invite Liam?' I asked.

'Of course you can,' said Mum.

'Tell him to meet us at the station,' said Dad. 'We don't have much time and I don't want to miss the train.'

We got to the station at a quarter to ten. But Liam wasn't there.

'Let's get a cup of coffee,' said Mum. Dad looked worried.

'All right,' he said. 'But be quick. I'll get the tickets.'

Dad had the tickets. Mum had her coffee. We had five minutes to get to platform 3. 'Let's take the stairs,' Dad said. 'They're quicker than the escalator.'

We got on the train and sat down. It was 10 o'clock. But Liam still wasn't there. A whistle blew. 'Just in time,' said Dad, but our train didn't move. I looked out the window. The train on platform 5 was leaving. Then, I saw Liam and his mum on that train. They were waving at us.

'Is this really our train?' I asked Dad. He didn't say anything. He never says anything when he makes a mistake.

1 The family wanted to go ______________________.

2 They took the ______________ because Dad didn't want to drive.

3 Dad said the train was at 10'clock from ______________________.

4 Mum wanted a ______________________ at the station.

5 They used the ______________________ to get to the platform.

6 Liam and his mum ______________ at the family from the train on platform 5.

1 060 Listen and tick ☑ the correct time.

2 Work with a friend. Look at the pictures. Make sentences.

When I went to the park, …

… a boy was drinking water.

Ways to travel

Watch and answer. How many types of transport do you know?

1 061 Listen and point.

road

fuel

electric train

electric car

2 Read and write the answer. Why are electric cars and trains eco-friendly?

There are lots of ways to travel. People can travel by plane, by train, by car and by ferry. Sometimes, these ways to travel are bad for the environment. That's because of the fuel they use to help them move.

Fuels often pollute the environment. Pollution is unhealthy for people and can be bad for land and sea habitats too. Walking, cycling and sailing are eco-friendly ways to travel because they don't need any fuel. *Eco-friendly* means that something is not bad for the environment. Cycling and walking are healthy ways to travel too, because they help you exercise.

Today, you can sometimes travel in electric cars, electric trains and electric buses. Electric transport is eco-friendly because it doesn't use fuel that pollutes the air. You can't travel by electric plane yet.

3 Write the numbers in the chart.

1 travelling on electric buses
2 travelling by plane
3 using cars with fuel, like oil
4 going by bike
5 walking
6 sailing

Eco-friendly	Not eco-friendly

4 Work with a friend. Answer the questions.

What's the most eco-friendly way you can:

- go on holiday?
- go to school?
- visit your friends?
- go to the town centre?

I can walk to school.

I can go to school by …

5 Look at the pictures and answer the questions. Talk to a partner.

1 Which pictures show fast ways to go to places?
2 Which pictures show healthy ways to go to places?
3 Which pictures show eco-friendly ways to go to places?

Pictures 1 and … show …

Super fact!

Electric cars aren't new. The first one was made more than 100 years ago.

6 Project Make an advertisement for one type of transport. Say why it's good to use it.

Talk and find out

At the train station

1 Choose a role card. Read and plan.

Student A

You want to go on a train trip. At the ticket office you tell the person where you want to go. You ask about:

- the price of a single ticket
- the price of a return ticket
- the time when the next train leaves
- the platform number
- the time when it arrives

Student B

You work at the ticket office. You tell the tourist:

- the price of a single ticket
- the price of a return ticket
- the time when the next train leaves
- the platform number
- the time when it arrives

Useful language

Tourist	Ticket office assistant
I want to go to …	
How much is a single ticket?	A single ticket is …
How much is a return ticket?	A return ticket is …
When does the train leave?	At …
When does it arrive?	At …
What platform number is it?	Platform …
Thank you very much.	You're welcome.

2 Act out your play.

Thank you very much.

A notice for a school trip

1 Read this notice from a school board. Tick ☑ the checklist and underline the information.

SCHOOL TRIP

We're going to visit Brighton on 2nd September.
Travel by train.
Meet outside the station at 8.30 am.
£7.50 per person (return).
The return train arrives at 5.30 pm.

CHECKLIST

Information to put in a notice about a school trip:

- where you're going to go ☐
- date ☐
- meeting point ☐
- meeting time ☐
- cost ☐
- return time ☐

2 Read these three notices. What information is missing from each one? Use the checklist in Activity 1 to help you.

SCHOOL TRIP

Join our trip.
Meet in front of the school.
Bring warm clothes and good shoes.
Cost per person £12.50.
Return to school at 4.30 pm.

Join us!

We're organising a trip to the Blue Lake. Meet at the bus stop in Green Lane at 9 o'clock on 5th October. Return to school at 5 o'clock.

We're going to visit London on 15th November.
Meet on platform 2 at the train station at 8 o'clock.
Price per person £9.

3 Write a notice for your school board. Use the checklist to help you.

Writing tip

After you write your notice, read it again to check you included all the information you need.

5 Police!

1 Listen and say the words. Then check with a friend. (062)

1 dark
2 curly
3 moustache
4 fair
5 scar
6 beard
7 blond
8 straight

BIG QUESTION How can we describe people?

2 (063) Listen and correct the sentences.

1 Grandpa was a teacher.
2 He chased a criminal for 30 years.
3 The criminal was very stupid.
4 Grandpa knows the criminal's name.

3 Play the describing game.

She's got short hair. It's curly and it's dark.

It's Ana.

1 064 Listen and number the pictures.

2 Put the words in order. Say the sentences.

1 police officer. used He to a be

2 used car. to He a fast drive

3 He to a walkie-talkie. used carry

4 used He chase criminals. dangerous to

3 065 Watch, listen and say.

Language focus

I **used to live** in an egg.
I **used to have** small legs.
I **used to sleep** next to my mum.
I **used to hold** her thumb.
I **used to get** scared at night.
But now I'm fine. I'm really all right.

4 Complete the sentences. Then compare with a partner.

1 I used to like … but I don't now!

2 I used to have … but I don't now!

3 I used to eat … but I don't now!

4 I used to be … but I'm not now!

I used to like finger painting.

Me too! / I didn't.

1 066 Listen and draw how Dad's hair used to be. Then sing the song.

I used to have some curly hair.
It was long and I dyed it fair.
I went down to the hairdresser's
And now there's nothing there.

Who are you?
Take a look.
I'm your dad.
No, you're NOT!

I used to have a big moustache,
Thick and dark – it was really smart.
And then I tried to cut it off,
But now there's just a scar.

Who are you? ...

I used to have a long brown beard,
But now it's in the bin.
I shaved it off the other day
And now there's just my chin.

Who are you? ... [x2]

Dad before

Dad now

2 Look at the pictures. How are these people different now?

Aunt Mary used to have …

Aunt Mary

before after

Uncle John

before after

Cousin Dave

before after

3 Think of someone you know well. How are they different now?

My dad used to have long black hair. Now it's short and grey.

1 068 Listen, read and circle.

1 Grandpa had to be careful because **there were lots of dangerous criminals** / **he had a dangerous dog**.

2 He didn't tell his wife anything because **he had to keep things secret** / **she wasn't interested**.

3 He had to wash his uniform every **week** / **day**.

4 Ben can't be a police officer because **his clothes are often dirty** / **he's too small**.

2 Where do the words go? Say the sentences.

1 We to wear a uniform. (had)

2 We had be really careful. (to)

3 We had to everything secret. (keep)

3 069 Watch, listen and say.

Language focus

A surprise party for Gina's birthday!
I **had to keep** it secret.
I **had to tell** her friends.
They **had to keep** it secret.
I **had to get** a cake.
I **had to put up** lights.
I **had to work** all night.
After lots and lots of work
Everything was right.

4 Imagine you went to the world's worst holiday camp. Why was it bad?

I had to wash up every day.
I had to get up at 5 am.

The Mysterious H

1 070 Look at pictures 1–4. What did the Mysterious H steal?

1

Grandpa: The Mysterious H started robbing jewellers. He used to steal necklaces, bracelets and watches. There wasn't a shop in London which was safe.

2

Grandpa: His next plans were cleverer. He stole famous paintings and works of art from museums all over the world.

3

Grandpa: Then he stole the Queen's crown. The story was in all the papers. I had to find this man quickly.

4

Grandpa: He went to Paris and stole the top of the Eiffel Tower too!

Lucy: What?

5

Ben: But Grandpa, how did you know it was the same man?

Grandpa: He used to leave us a note. It always had the same symbol on it – the letter *H*.

6

Lucy: Did you catch him?

Grandpa: No. We almost caught him once, but he escaped.

7

Ben: It's a great story, but I don't understand. What's the connection with the waiter at the restaurant?

8

Grandpa: Ah, the waiter was wearing a ring with the letter *H* ... the same *H* that was on the notes ... that the Mysterious H used to leave.

Ben and Lucy: Wow!

2 Read and write *t* (true) or *f* (false).

1 The Mysterious H robbed jewellers all over London. ☐
2 He only robbed places in England. ☐
3 He stole the Queen's ring. ☐
4 The Mysterious H went to Paris. ☐
5 He always left the police a note. ☐
6 The waiter in the restaurant had an *M* on his ring. ☐

Phonics

3 Find the car and the horse in the story.

4 071 Listen and say.

My horse is short and dark with an awful scar.

1 **Look at the pictures in Activity 2. Answer the questions.**

1 Who do you think the Gentleman Robber was?

2 What did he steal?

2 072 **Read and listen. Check your answers.**

The Gentleman Robber

One day a man walked into a jeweller's shop. He was tall with short blond hair. He had a moustache and a beard and a small scar on his face. He wanted to buy a watch and he asked the woman in the shop to show him the most expensive watch they had. The woman showed him the watch. He looked at the watch, then he said to the lady, 'I'm very sorry but I'm going to rob you.' He put the watch in his pocket and ran out of the shop.

The lady was shocked. She called the police and told them everything.

A few months later, the police got a phone call from another jeweller in the same town. They went to the shop and talked to the man who worked there.

'I was working in the shop when a man came in,' he said. 'He was tall with short blond hair. He had a moustache and a beard and a small scar on his right cheek. He wanted to buy a necklace for his wife. I showed him the most expensive one we had. Then he said, "I'm very sorry but I'm going to rob you," and ran out of my shop.' The police thought it was the same man. They gave him a name, the Gentleman Robber, because he always said 'sorry'.

Over the next year, the Gentleman Robber robbed four more jewellers. The police artist talked to all the shop workers and he drew a picture. It was of a tall man with short blond hair, a moustache and a beard, and a small scar on his right cheek. The police put the picture in the newspaper and asked people who knew the man to phone them.

A few days later they got a phone call. The man they were looking for was a doctor. The police arrested the man. No one who knew the doctor believed he was the robber. It was impossible. The doctors who worked with him said, 'He's a good man! He helps people.' But when the shop workers looked at him, they all agreed. He was the Gentleman Robber. Soon the doctor was in prison.

Only one person knew the mistake the police made – the real Gentleman Robber. He read about the doctor in the newspaper. The next day he walked into a jeweller's but he didn't rob it. He said, 'Tell the police they've got the wrong man.' He then gave the shop owner the watch from his very first robbery. When they saw the watch, the police knew their mistake and they let the doctor out of prison. The Gentleman Robber never robbed another jeweller. The police never caught him and to this day, nobody knows who he is.

3 Complete the sentences.

1 The robber had a scar on ____________________.

2 In the first shop he took ____________________.

3 The woman in the shop called ____________________.

4 In the second shop he took ____________________.

5 The police called him the Gentleman Robber because ____________________.

6 The police arrested a ____________________.

7 All the shop workers said the doctor was ____________________.

8 The police never caught ____________________.

4 073 Listen to a summary of the story. Write the four differences.

In the summary we have …

1 crown instead of necklace.

2 ________ instead of ________.

3 ________ instead of ________.

4 ________ instead of ________.

5 Imagine and draw another robber. Write a sentence to describe them.

Sketches

Watch and answer. How can we make sketches of people?

1 074 Listen and point.

sketch

shading

curved line

dark line

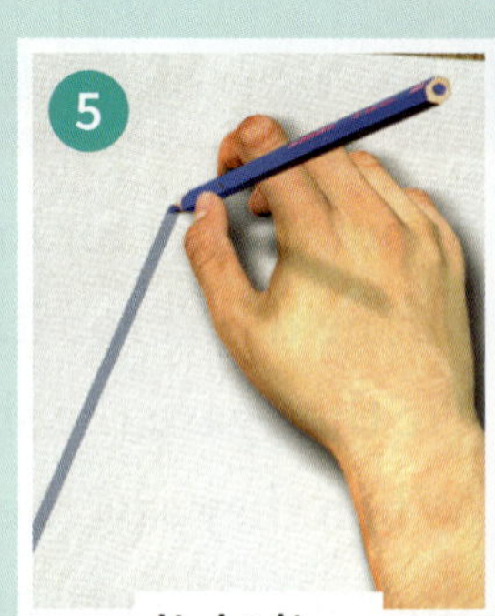
light line

2 Look at this sketch. Write the numbers in the boxes.

1 straight lines
2 curved, dark lines
3 shading
4 light lines

Super fact!

Sometimes artists make sketches of criminals to help the police find them.

3 Imagine the man was wearing glasses and had a scar on his nose. What kind of lines would you sketch to show the glasses and scar? Draw them in the picture.

4 Read about how artists draw sketches. Then match the materials with the lines.

Artists use different materials to draw sketches. They can use pencils, pens, crayons and charcoal. Sometimes artists use two or three different materials in the same sketch and use different coloured paper. Sometimes they work on a computer to do a sketch.

1 pencil ☐
2 pen ☐
3 crayon ☐
4 charcoal ☐

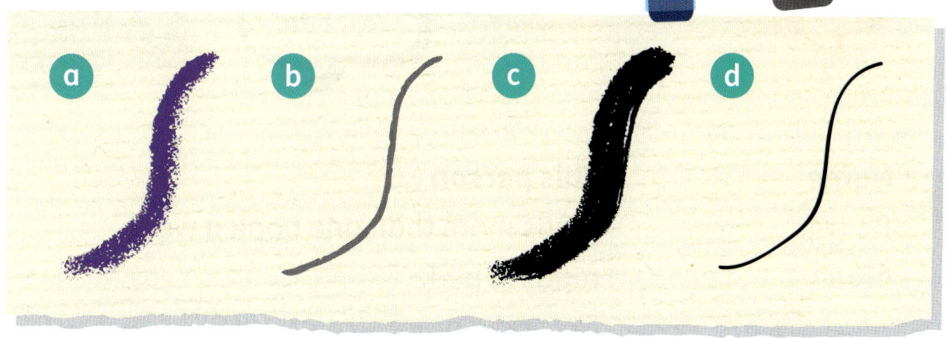

5 Look at the sketches and read the description. Which sketch is it? Talk to your partner about the other three sketches.

This sketch has got lots of yellow shading. The artist used yellow and white crayons on black paper.

This sketch …

6 Project Make a sketch of your friend. Write a description of your sketch.

This sketch has got lots of shading and curved lines. I used grey and brown pencils on white paper.

Talk and find out

Reading habits

1 Ask questions and write names.

David, do you read more than one book a week?

No, I don't.

Elena, do you read in bed?

Yes, I do.

Name	This person ...
Pedro	reads more than one book a week.
Elena	reads in bed.
	likes adventure stories.
	likes funny stories.
	reads comics.
	doesn't like crime stories.
	's parents have got books in other languages at home.
	doesn't use a library outside school.
	hasn't got a book of poems.
	prefers reading to computer games.

2 Work in groups. Talk about what you found out.

Toni reads in bed.

Luca likes funny stories.

A book review

1 Read the two book reviews. Which one is better? Why?

a

BOOK REVIEW

'A true friend' by RJ Glass. This book is about Erin. She hasn't got any friends. Then she gets some friends. I liked this book.

b

Book review

'A true friend' by **RJ Glass**. This book is about a girl called Erin. Erin hasn't got many friends because she is shy. One day a new student arrives at Erin's school and her life is never the same again. I liked this book because it was very exciting.

2 Use the notes to write a review.

Book:	The Clown
Author:	Robert Wise
Main character:	Jim / popular / very funny
What happens?	forgets how to laugh / loses his friends
What did I think?	good / sad

3 Think of a book and make notes.

4 Write a review. Draw the cover.

Book:
Author:
Main character:
What happens?
What did I think?

Writing tip

Don't say what happens at the end of the story in your book review!

6 Mythical beasts

1 075 **Listen and say the words. Then check with a friend.**

1 wing
2 horn
3 back
4 scales
5 neck
6 tail
7 feathers
8 tongue

BIG QUESTION What were animals like long ago?

2 076 **Listen and answer.**

1 How did Ben know about the dragon?
2 What is Ben holding?
3 Why is this the right place?
4 Where do they look last?

3 **Play the animal game.**

I'm thinking of an animal. Can you guess?

Has it got wings?

Can it … ?

1 077 Read and write *t* (true) or *f* (false). Then listen and check.

Dino facts – or dino myths?

1 The biggest dinosaur was longer than ten cars. ☐
2 The fastest dinosaurs could run at 60 km/h. ☐
3 T-Rex was one of the most dangerous dinosaurs. ☐
4 The heaviest dinosaur was more than 80,000 kilos. ☐
5 The best dinosaur film is called *Planet of Dinosaurs*. ☐
6 The worst dinosaur film is called *Legend of the Dinosaurs*. ☐

2 Put the words in order. Say the sentences.

1 heaviest the The was dinosaur. Argentinosaurus
2 is cheetah than faster The the T-Rex.

3 078 Watch, listen and say.

Language focus

Who's **the most dangerous** animal in this park?
It's **bigger than** a crocodile. It's this shark!
Who's **the best** dancer at this zoo?
She's **better than** the lion.
It's … well, it's you!
Who's **the worst** singer in this house?
It's **worse than** a tiger. It's this mouse!

Who's **the prettiest** animal in this tree?
He's **more beautiful than** a fish.
It's … well, it's me!

4 Work in groups. Write six sentences for an animal quiz. Then test your friends.

A correct sentence = 1 point   Only your group writes this sentence = 3 points

African elephants are bigger than Indian elephants   True / False
Cats are friendlier than dogs.   True / False

1 079 Listen and match the names with the animals. Then sing the song.

1

2

3

a Megalodon
b Gastornis
c Titanoboa

My favourite book is my dinosaur book.
It's the best book without a doubt.
When I open the pages of my dinosaur book,
The animals jump right out.

The Titanoboa was a very long snake.
It's the longest snake in my book,
With scales from its head right down to its tail.
Please come and have a look.

My favourite book is my dinosaur book ...

The Megalodon was a very scary shark.
It's the scariest shark in my book,
With a giant fin along its back.
Please come and have a look.

My favourite book is my dinosaur book ...

The Gastornis was a very big bird.
It's the biggest bird in my book,
With very big feathers and a very strong tongue.
Please come and have a look.

2 Play the animal game. Think of an animal. The others have to find out what it is.

Has it got wings / sharp teeth / a tail / a long tongue ... ?

Does it live in Brazil / Spain / Mexico ... ?

Can it fly / swim / climb trees ... ?

Does it eat ... ?

Is it a ... ?

3 Write a new verse about the Smilodon.

The Smilodon ...

1 081 Look at the beasts. Write the names under the pictures. Listen and check.

Pegasus the Sphinx a mermaid a unicorn the Phoenix a centaur

Did you know? Around the world there are lots of stories about mythical beasts. These beasts often look like animals, but sometimes they are half animal and half human.

1 

2 

3 

4 

5 

6 

2 Complete with *looks* or *like*. Say the sentences.

1 The Sphinx like a lion.

2 A unicorn looks a white horse.

3 082 Watch, listen and say.

Language focus

What **does** a polligecko **look like**?
It **looks like** a gecko, but it's got a parrot's head.

What **does** a geckodile **look like**?
It **looks like** a gecko with a crocodile's head.

4 Take it in turns to close your book. Ask and answer.

geckofish

tigergecko

geckorat

spidergecko

What does the geckofish look like?

It looks like a gecko with a fish's tail.

The secret door

1 083 How do Ben and Lucy get out of the statue?

Lucy: Ben, come over here.
Ben: What is it?

Lucy: Look. There's a little door. Let's open it.
Ben: Good idea. Let's see what's inside.

Ben: I hope it's not a trap!
Lucy: Me too! Now, let's start looking for that line.

Horax: Now we've got you! Give us the map or you have to stay in there forever!

Ben: We can't get out of that door. What can we do?
Lucy: Hmm, look! There's a ladder. Maybe it's a way out. It's our best chance!

Lucy: We can get out here. Let's jump into the pool, but be careful with the map!
Ben: It's in my jacket. I just hope that Horax and Zelda aren't looking.

7

Lucy: They're still there! But they can't see us.
Ben: Hey, look here – on the side of the pool!
Lucy: It's the next line: 'Look down and find the treasure chest'. Great! Now let's go. Hurry up!

8

Ben: Lucy, run!
Zelda: Oh, no. Look!
Horax: Stop, you two! We're going to get you!

2 Read and make sentences.

1 Lucy finds
2 They leave the door open
3 Horax
4 When Horax closes the door,
5 Lucy has an idea how
6 The map doesn't get wet

a when they go down the stairs.
b because it's in Ben's jacket.
c shuts the door.
d a way into the dragon.
e he is sure he is going to get the map.
f to get out of the dragon.

Phonics

3 Find the feathers on the beast in the story.

4 084 Listen and say.

Heather's bird has heavy feathers and eats a lot of meat and beans.

1 085 Listen and tick ☑ the correct picture.

1 Where did Paul find the book?

2 Where did the dinosaurs in the book live?

3 What did they eat?

4 What happened to the book?

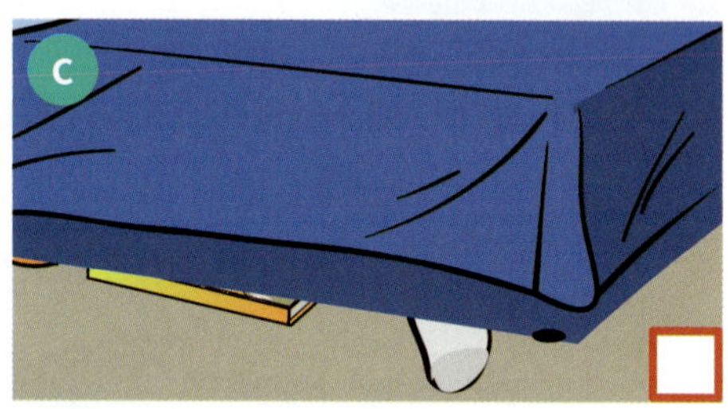

5 What did Paul give his sister?

1 Work with a friend. What happens in each picture? Make a list of words for each picture.

1

2

3

4

2 Tell the story with a friend.

One day Shelly and her friends were in the park. They …

3 Now write the story.

One day Shelly and her friends were …

Shelly … She …

In the morning …

It had …

A week later …

Dinosaurs

Watch and answer. What were dinosaurs like?

Super fact!

People who know a lot about dinosaurs are called *palaeontologists*. It's a very long word – try to say it!

1 086 Listen and point.

1 tyrannosaurus

2 stegosaurus

3 oviraptor

4 beak

2 Read about three different dinosaurs. Make notes to complete the chart.

The tyrannosaurus was a very big dinosaur with lots of sharp teeth. It had a big head and two small arms and it could run quickly on its two legs. Palaeontologists think that it ate smaller dinosaurs.

The stegosaurus was a dinosaur that had smaller teeth than a tyrannosaurus. It was as big as a bus and moved on four legs. Its head was small and it ate plants.

The oviraptor was a dinosaur that ate plants, eggs, insects and meat. It was a small dinosaur with two long legs and two long arms. Its head looked a bit like a bird and it didn't have any teeth. It used its beak to eat food.

	What was its head like?	What were its teeth like?	How many arms and legs?	What food did it eat?
tyrannosaurus	big			
stegosaurus				
oviraptor				

3 Read about what different animals eat. Match each text with a dinosaur from Activity 1.

HERBIVORES

Herbivores are animals like giraffes that eat plants, not meat. Their teeth are flat so they can pull leaves from trees. Herbivores eat more than carnivores because they need to eat lots of plant parts so they can grow.

____

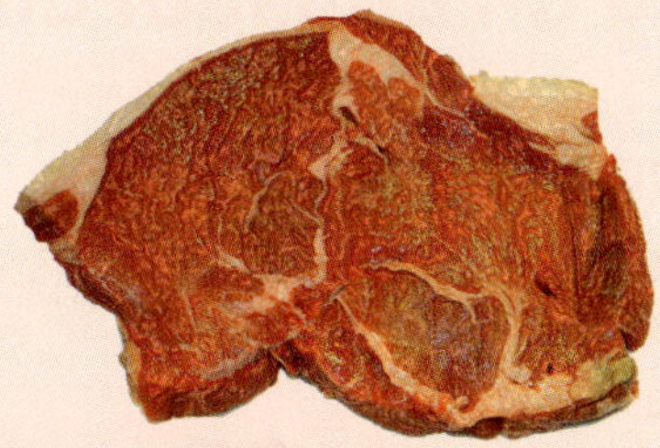

CARNIVORES

Carnivores are animals that eat meat, like lions and snakes. Carnivores have got strong teeth and can move fast to catch other animals.

____

OMNIVORES

Omnivores are animals that eat meat, eggs, insects and plants, like some birds.

____

4 Think of two more animals for each category.

1 Herbivores: ____________________ ____________________

2 Carnivores: ____________________ ____________________

3 Omnivores: ____________________ ____________________

5 Project Make a dinosaur information card. Find out about another kind of dinosaur and draw a picture. Write some information about it.

The triceratops had a very big head and three horns. It had lots of teeth and moved on four legs. It was a herbivore.

Talk and find out

Finding an unusual animal

1 Choose a role card. Read and plan.

Student A

You are in the park and you see a very unusual animal. Think about the following:

- What does it look like?
- Has it got (wings / fur / claws …)?
- Can it (swim / fly / run very fast …)?

Now phone the zoo. Tell the director about the animal and ask what you should do.

Student B

You are the zoo director. Someone is going to phone you to tell you about an unusual animal. Think about what you want to know:

- Looks?
- What can it do?

Make a decision about what to do.

Useful language

Finder	**Director**
Hello, am I talking to the director of the zoo? I've got a strange animal. It looks like … It's got … It can … It's faster than / bigger than / smaller than …	What exactly does it look like? What colour is it? Has it got … ? How big … ?

2 Act out your play.

Think and write

My beast

1 **Read Ryan's text. Add eight full stops.** • full stop

This was the unicornix It lived a million years ago and it was the heaviest animal in those days It was pink and it looked like a horse It had a big horn on its head It also had wings with lots of beautiful feathers They were green and gold The unicornix could fly and it was faster than the fastest bird It could also swim and run and it was one of the most dangerous animals in the world

2 **Read Tammy's text. Add capital letters and seven full stops.**

the minirex was the smallest dinosaur in the world it was smaller than a mouse it was half dinosaur and half bird and it also looked like a fish it had horns and wings the wings had feathers its tail was long and full of scales it was the fastest animal under water

Writing tip

Read your text aloud to check. Pause after each full stop.

3 **Imagine and draw a mythical beast. Write about it.**

- What was its name?
- When did it live?
- What did it look like? (Another animal? Did it have horns / wings / feathers / a tail / scales … ?)
- Was it heavier or smaller than other animals? Was it the biggest, the fastest … ?
- What could it do? (Fly? Swim? Run very fast … ?)

7 Orchestra practice

1 Ⓒ 087 **Listen and say the words. Then check with a friend.**

1 trombone
2 triangle
3 keyboard
4 drums
5 tambourine
6 saxophone
7 trumpet
8 violin
9 harp

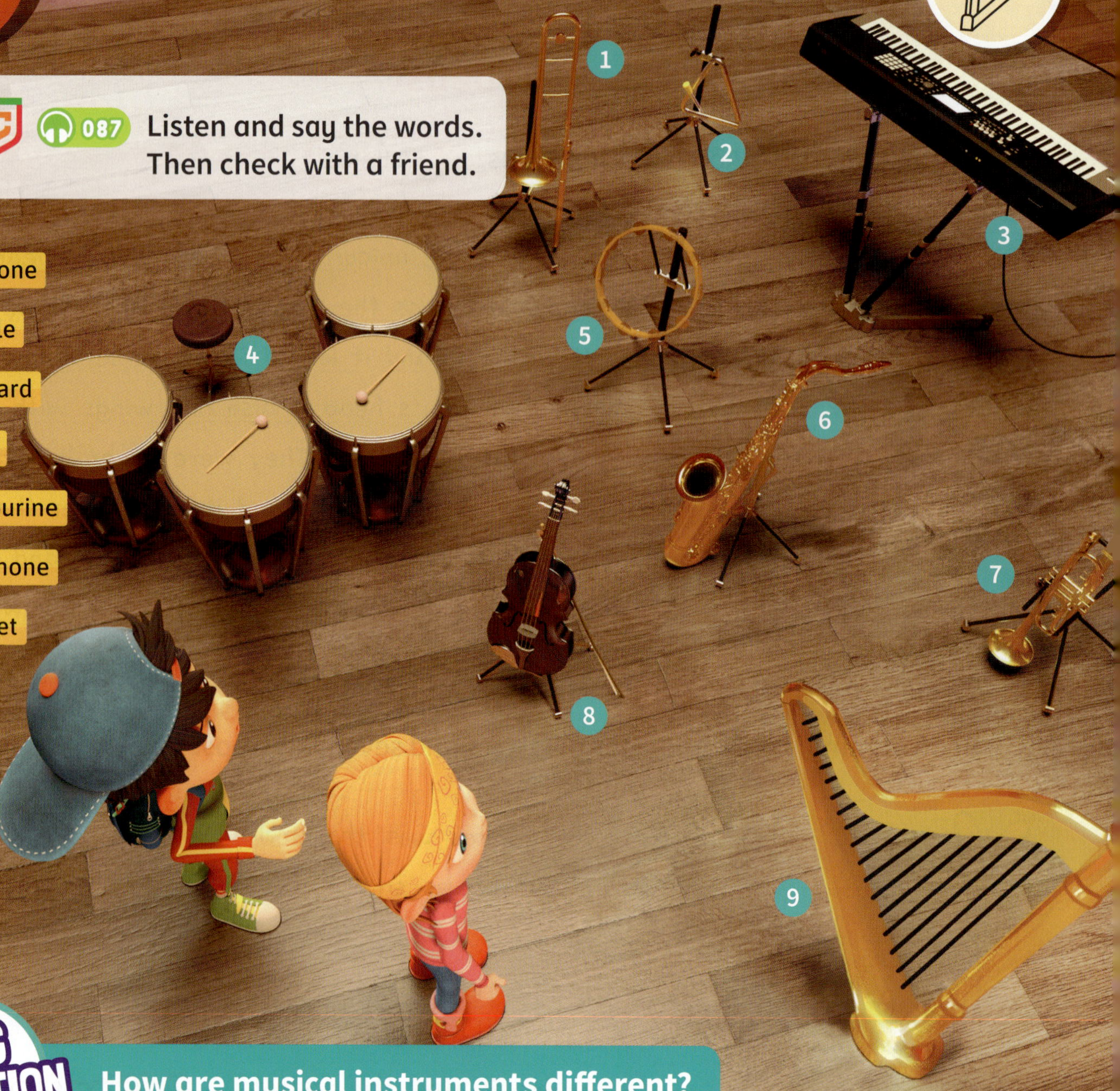

BIG QUESTION How are musical instruments different?

2 088 **Listen and correct the sentences.**

1 Lucy and Ben arrive last.
2 Ben knows other musical places.
3 They check six instruments.
4 They can look again at lunchtime.

3 **Play the miming game. Ask and answer.**

Are you playing the violin?

Yes, I am.

1 089 **Listen and write the names.**

Theo Jade Rosy Tom Hannah

1 ________
2 ________
3 ________

4 ________
5 ________

2 **Complete with the words from the box. Say the sentences.**

hers yours ours mine theirs his

1 It's my guitar. = It's ________.
2 It's your guitar. = It's ________.
3 It's his guitar. = It's ________.
4 It's her guitar. = It's ________.
5 It's our guitar. = It's ________.
6 It's their guitar. = It's ________.

3 090 **Watch, listen and say.**

Language focus

Is this **yours**, Greg?	No, it's not **mine**.	Is this **theirs**, Greg?	I don't know.
Is this **his**, Greg?	No, it's not **his**.	Is this **yours**?	No, it's not **ours**.
Is this **hers**, Greg?	No, it's not **hers**.	Is this **yours**, Gina?	Yes, it's **mine**!

4 **Play the *Whose instrument is it?* game.**

1 091 Listen and match the children with their instruments. Then sing the song.

1  Kate

2  Dave

3  Tim

4  Hope

We start with the drums
in our song.
Dave is the drummer
in the band,
And the drums that
he's playing are his.
We're the best band in the land.

Next comes the keyboard in our song.
Kate plays the keyboard in the band.
The keyboard that she's
playing is hers.
We're the best band
in the land.

It's time for the harp in
our song.
Hope is the harpist
in the band,
And the harp that
she's playing is hers.
We're the best band in the land.

And here comes the trumpet in our song.
I play the trumpet in the band.
The trumpet that I'm playing is mine.
We're the best band in the land.

Oops! I forgot to say that
Tim is my name.

2 What instruments do these children play? (Clue – look carefully at the names)

~~Tammy~~ Sarah Trixie Vincent Troy

Tammy

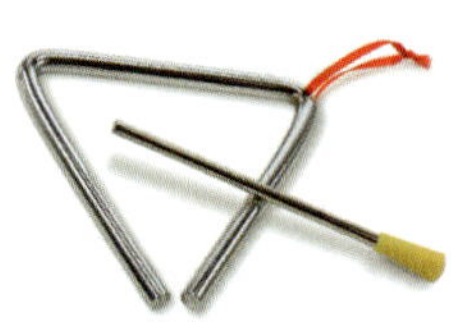

3 What instrument would you like to play in the orchestra?

I'd like to play the triangle because it isn't very heavy.

1 093 **Listen and match the children with the instruments and the houses.**

Vicky | Christina | Claire | Connor | Josh | Mark

2 Where do the words go? Say the sentences.

1 Ollie is the boy plays the trumpet. (who)

2 The house I live is blue. (where)

3 The instrument I play is the guitar. (which)

3 094 **Watch, listen and say.**

Language focus

I am the gecko **who** plays guitar.

The songs **which** I sing have awesome words.

The place **where** I play is really cool.

4 Look at the pictures. Follow the lines and make sentences.

The instrument which Shona plays is …

The house where …

At the concert hall

1 095 Where does Horax hide the map?

1

Conductor: OK, time for a break. You can all go to the café now and have a drink and a snack.

Ben: Shall we stay here and look for the line?

2

Lucy: Let's go for a drink first. I'm thirsty.

Ben: I'm hungry too. We can look later.

Lucy: Good idea.

3

Ben: Orange juice and an apple, please.

Lucy: And hot chocolate and a banana for me, please.

Assistant: Here you are.

4

Ben: Hey, I can see something which you can't … the line! It's on your cup!

Lucy: Is it? Well spotted! What does it say?

Ben: 'In the lighthouse you will see'.

5

Horax: Ha! Here's the map which is going to make me rich and famous. I knew it! Very nice of you, kids. Thank you.

6

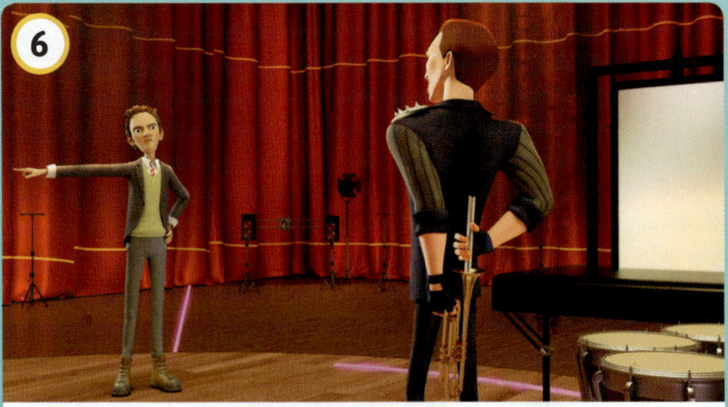

Conductor: What are you doing in here? It's the junior orchestra. You shouldn't be here.

Horax: Erm … I'm sorry, I'm so sorry.

Conductor: Leave now! Before I call the police.

Lucy: Oh, no! Look! Your rucksack's open.
Ben: The map! Where is it? Horax! He was here!
Lucy: Oh, no! We can't do anything now. We have to play.

Lucy: Hey, there's the map!
Ben: Cool!

2 **Cover the story. Complete the sentences.**

1 Lucy and Ben play in ____________________

2 Lucy plays ____________________ and Ben plays ____________________

3 During the break they ____________________

4 In the café they find ____________________

5 When they come back, they ____________________

6 The map ____________________

Phonics

3 **Find the girl with short curly hair in the orchestra.**

4 096 **Listen and say.**

Fern is tall and works with the birds in the orchestra.

1 Look at the pictures in Activity 2. Which instruments can you see?

2 097 Read and listen. Who plays the most important note?

TRISTAN AND THE TRIANGLE

It was Monday morning. The musicians in the orchestra were very excited. The conductor had some new music for them. They had five days to learn it for the big concert on Friday. The conductor gave each musician their music. They looked at the music to see how many notes they had to play.

The trumpet player was the first to speak. ‘Look at all my notes!’ he shouted. ‘I play a loud and important instrument. When I play, people are happy.’

The violin player spoke next. ‘I’ve got lots of notes to play,’ she said. ‘My notes are soft. When people hear my violin, they feel relaxed.’

‘I’ve got lots of notes too,’ said the trombone player. ‘My notes are deep. When I play the trombone, people dance.’

Finally, the drummer spoke. ‘When I play my notes on the drums,’ she said, ‘people feel excited!’

One by one, all the musicians talked about how important they were. But the triangle player, Tristan, was quiet and sad. He looked at the music in front of him. There was only one note for him to play. Just one little note! It was the last note of the music.

All week the musicians practised. Each day the musicians played louder and louder. They all wanted to be the most important instrument in the orchestra. Tristan sat and watched them all.

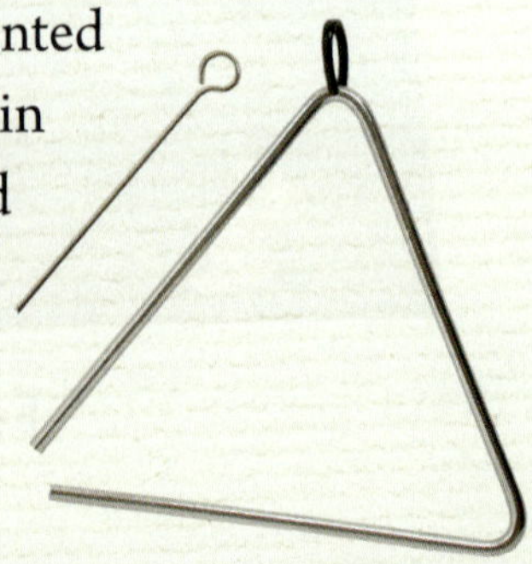

Then it was Friday evening. All the musicians sat in their chairs with their instruments. They were all very excited. There were hundreds of people in the big hall in front of them. The conductor walked onto the stage. He hit his baton on his head, put his arms up high and then the music started.

The trumpet was loud, the drums were louder, and the violin was soft and beautiful. Tristan just sat and waited with his triangle in his hands. He watched all the other musicians. He counted the notes one by one until there was only one note left on the paper. The hall was silent. No trumpets, no drums, no violins, no trombone.

'Ting!' Tristan's one little note rang through the hall. Then everyone stood up from their chairs and started cheering. 'Hurray,' they shouted. 'Hurray!'

The conductor walked past the trumpet players and the trombone players. He walked past the drum and violin players. He walked up to Tristan. 'Thank you,' he said. 'Thank you! That was the most important note in the music.'

3 **Complete the sentences.**

1 The concert was on …
2 The second musician to speak was …
3 Tristan only had …
4 On the day of the concert the musicians were …
5 Tristan played the last …
6 The conductor thanked …

4 098 **Listen to a summary of the story. Write the four differences.**

In the summary we have …

1 Saturday instead of Friday.
2 ________ instead of ________.
3 ________ instead of ________.
4 ________ instead of ________.

5 **How do you think Tristan felt at the end of the concert? Complete his diary.**

12th April

Today was our school concert. Before the concert, I felt ________ because I didn't have many notes to play. But after the concert the conductor said 'thank you' to me and said that my note was the most important in the music. I felt ________ and ________.

Instrument FAMILIES

Watch and answer. How do we play instruments?

Super fact!

Playing the drums can be very good exercise. Drumming for an hour can be better exercise than cycling or hiking for an hour.

1 099 Listen and point.

1

bow

string instruments

2

recorder

wind instruments

3

percussion instruments

4

pluck

5

blow

6

hit

7

shake

8

musician

2 Read and circle the ten instrument words. Can you play any of them? Which ones would you like to play? Tell your friend.

Percussion instruments

Musicians hit percussion instruments, like drums and triangles, to make sounds. They play other percussion instruments, like tambourines, by shaking or hitting them.

String instruments

Musicians pluck string instruments, like guitars and harps, to make short sounds. They use a bow to make long sounds with instruments like violins.

Wind instruments

Musicians blow into wind instruments, like trumpets, trombones and recorders. When they blow a lot, the instruments sound very noisy but when they only blow a little, the instruments sound quiet.

Pianos

Pianos have got strings too. The strings are inside the piano. Musicians hit the black and white keys with their fingers. These keys then hit the strings in the piano. So a piano is a percussion instrument and a string instrument.

keys

I can play the triangle. I'd like to play the piano.

3 Look at the instruments you circled in Activity 2. Put the percussion and string instruments into different groups in the Venn diagram.

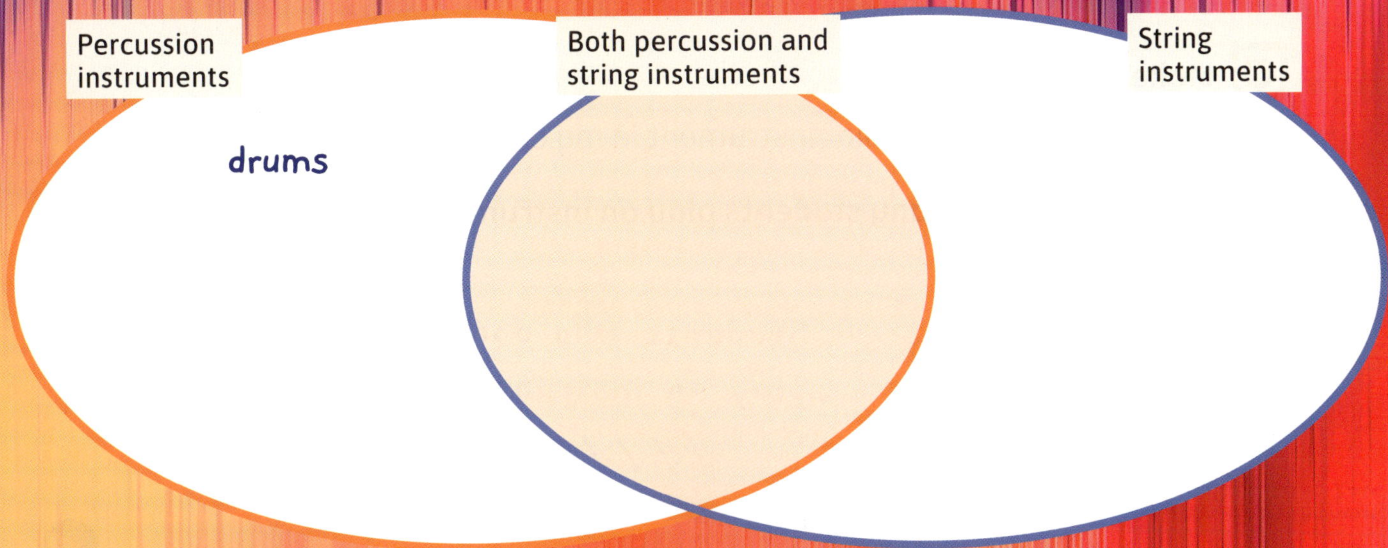

4 Look at this Carroll diagram. Which musical instruments go into the three boxes?

drum triangle tambourine piano

	Percussion instrument	String instrument
Hit		
Shake		

5 Project Make a Carroll diagram with types of musical instruments.

	String instrument	Not string instrument
Pluck	guitar, harp, violin	
Don't pluck	piano 	trumpet, trombone, recorder, drum, tambourine, triangle 

Talk and find out

Music in our class

1 **Make a prediction.**

I predict that the most popular instrument in my class is the ________.

2 **Work in groups. How many students play an instrument? What instruments do they play?**

Students who play an instrument	Students who don't play an instrument	Instruments
✓✓✓	✓✓✓✓	recorder ✓✓ guitar ✓

3 **Ask the students who don't play an instrument: Would you like to play an instrument? Which one?**

Would like to play an instrument ✓✓	Wouldn't like to play an instrument ✓✓
drums ✓ saxophone ✓	

4 **Find out about your class.**

- favourite singer
- favourite band
- favourite song
- a song you really don't like

5 **Write the results on the board. Then write a report.**

Music in our class

I predicted that the most popular instrument in my class is the recorder. In my class, 8 children play the recorder, and 2 children would like to play the recorder. So now I know that my prediction is correct. My class's favourite singer is Ariana Grande. 10 children like her. Our favourite band is Little Mix. A song we really don't like is 'Idol' by BTS. Only Chloe likes BTS! Our favourite song is 'Power'.

My music review

1 Read Shannan's text. Look at the highlighted words. Write the short forms.

I love music. My favourite (1) (2) She is 24 years old and (3) she is an excellent singer. My favourite Laura Gold (4) song is 'Goodbye'. I often listen to it before I fall asleep. (5) She has also got a song called 'Paper flowers'. (6) It is fantastic. Now (7) Laura has got a new song, 'Sweet dreams'. (8) I do not think (9) it is very good because she sings without a band.

1 ________ 6 ________
2 ________ 7 ________
3 ________ 8 ________
4 ________ 9 ________
5 ________

2 Write Tyler's text again. Use short forms.

I have not got a favourite singer, but I have got a favourite band. They are called 4by4. Nick is the drummer. Sharon and Rick play the guitar. Keith plays the trumpet. Their most successful song is 'Dancing in the sunset'. I love it because the words are really cool. The music is good too. My sister has got a poster of the band on her bedroom wall!

3 Think of your favourite band or singer. Write a text using short forms. Add photos or drawings.

- name
- why you like him / her / them
- favourite song(s)
- why you like it / them

Writing tip

Remember to use apostrophes to show that letters are missing from the short forms.

8 In the planetarium

1 100 Listen and say the words. Then check with a friend.

1 comet
2 star
3 UFO
4 rocket
5 planet
6 moon
7 telescope
8 astronaut
9 space station

BIG QUESTION Why is space exciting?

2 101 Listen and answer.

1 Who is Ben calling?
2 Is Grandpa at the planetarium?
3 What question does Ben answer?
4 Where is the telescope?

3 Describe and guess.

It's something which you use to look at the stars.

A telescope!

It's someone who …

1 102 Listen and write the names of the children under the pictures.

Nathan Oscar Liam Jade Emily Daisy

a

______

b

______

c
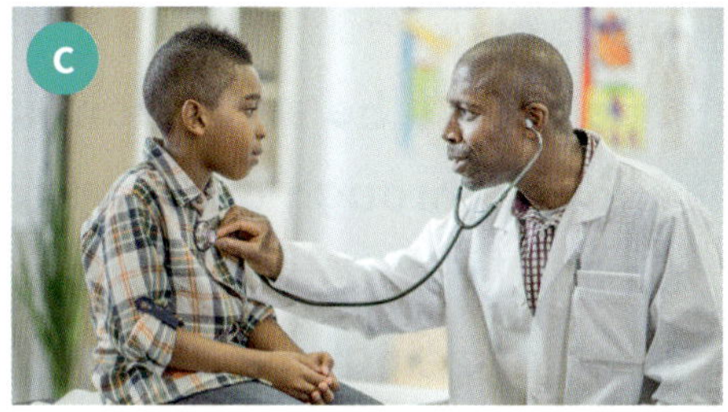
______

d

______

e

______

f

______

2 Where do the words go? Say the sentences.

1 What you be when you grow up? (will)

2 I be a zoo keeper. I look after the lions. ('ll, 'll)

3 103 Watch, listen and say.

Language focus

When I grow up, **I'll be** a spy.
Shh! It's secret. Don't ask why.
I'll have a special mobile phone.

You'll never **find** me at my home.
I'll have a very special car.
It'll travel to the stars.

4 Ask and answer.

What will you be when you grow up?

I'll be a conductor because I love music. I'll have a big orchestra.

1 104 Listen and number the pictures. Then sing the song.

10, 9, 8, 7, 6, 5, 4, 3, 2, 1 and blast off!
One day I'll be an astronaut
And fly through outer space.
I'll live in a space station
In an exciting place.

I'll climb inside a rocket
And fly up to the moon
And whizz about in outer space
And not come back too soon.

One day I'll be an astronaut …

I'll fly up on a comet
And hold on to its tail
And whizz about in outer space
And look back at our trail.

One day I'll be an astronaut …

I'll visit lots of planets
Like Jupiter and Mars
And whizz about in outer space
And visit all the stars.

One day I'll be an astronaut …

10, 9, 8, 7, 6, 5, 4, 3, 2, 1 stop!

a

b

c

2 Imagine you live in space. Make a list of six exciting things you'll do.

1 Get a space pet 2 Eat space food 3 …

3 Tell your friend about your plans.

I'll get a space pet.

1 Look, read and number the sentences.

a The astronaut put on his spacesuit carefully. ☐

b He opened the space station door slowly. ☐

c He stepped through the door quietly. ☐

d Whoops! Wrong door! ☐

2 Put the words in order. Say the sentences.

1 food carefully. astronaut The ate her

2 quietly. The through travelled spaceship space

3 rocket the left quickly. moon The

3 ▶ 🎧 106 Watch, listen and say.

Language focus

How do you catch a fly?
Listen **carefully**.
Find a fly **quietly**.

Open your mouth **slowly**.
Then shoot your tongue out **quickly**.
That's how you catch a fly!

4 Give a friend instructions with adverbs.

Put your book on your head carefully.

Touch your nose quickly three times.

Walk to the door slowly.

Sing a song quietly.

The trap

1 107 Who takes Horax and Zelda to the police station?

1

Lucy: I can't see a line anywhere.

Ben: No. I don't think it's here. Let's go for a drink and we can think about it.

Lucy: Good idea.

2

Horax: 'Look at the planets, look at the stars.' Ha! Stupid kids. The line will be on this map!

Zelda: Ah! Look! A poem! I'll read it.

3

Zelda: 'Off to the moon we go for a ride. Go over there and climb inside. There you'll find the final line. Find my treasure with this rhyme.'

4

Horax: That's easy. It's inside the rocket! Come on! Let's look carefully.

Zelda: The treasure is almost ours!

5

Horax: Hey, what's happening? ... Oh, those kids!

Lucy: It was a trick. We knew you were here!

Ben: And I knew you were listening to my phone call. There *isn't* a planet on the map.

6

Lucy: And there *isn't* a line here. We wrote the note and the poem to trick you!

Horax: Let us out!

Ben: I can't. But here's someone who can.

 Value: respecting your elders; reading for pleasure

7

Ben: Grandpa! Your plan worked perfectly.

Grandpa: I knew it! My friend is going to take Horax and Zelda to the police station. He's got a lot of questions for them.

8

Ben: Now we can find the last line with no more trouble.

Grandpa: And maybe I will find the answer to a mystery of my own.

2 **Answer the questions.**

1 Did Ben and Lucy know that Horax and Zelda were there? ____________

2 Where does Zelda find a poem? ____________

3 Who wrote the poem? ____________

4 What do Horax and Zelda want to find in the rocket? ____________

5 What are the police going to do at the police station? ____________

6 What is Grandpa's mystery? What do you think? ____________

Phonics

3 **Find the ladder in the story.**

4 108 **Listen and say.**

I want to be a surfer on Jupiter in outer space.

1 109 **Listen, colour and write.**

2 **Look at the picture in Activity 1 and read. Write *yes* or *no*.**

1 There are three windows in the rocket. ______
2 The aliens have got three eyes. ______
3 The astronaut is scared. ______
4 It is raining and the aliens are holding an umbrella. ______
5 The astronaut has got a flag in both hands. ______
6 The astronaut is shaking hands with the fattest alien. ______

1 Ask and answer. Find six differences.

Is there a planet in your picture?

Yes, there is.

2 Read Leo's email. Then complete his parents' conversation.

Dear Mum and Dad,

I'm having a wonderful time here on the moon. The journey here was quite long. It was about two days, but I slept most of the way. I like the space station. It's really big and there's lots to do. The only thing which isn't very good is the food.

I'll be home in a month.

Lots of love,

Leo

Mum: We've got an email from Leo!

Dad: **(1)** ______________________?

Mum: On the moon. Don't you remember?

Dad: Oh, yes! **(2)** ______________________?

Mum: About two days.

Dad: **(3)** ______________________?

Mum: Yes, he does. It's big and there's lots to do.

Dad: **(4)** ______________________?

Mum: No, it isn't. It isn't very good at all!

Dad: **(5)** ______________________?

Mum: In a month.

3 Imagine you're on the moon. Write an email to your parents.

Space

Watch and answer. What can we find in Space?

1 110 Listen and point.

1 heat

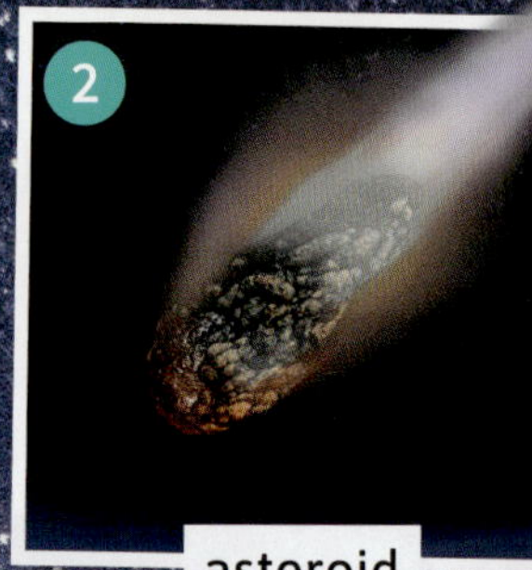

2 asteroid

3 planet Earth

4 orbit

5 planet Mars

6 the International Space Station

2 Read and write *t* (true) or *f* (false).

ALL ABOUT Space!

Space Space is very quiet because we can't hear sounds there. Astronauts have to use walkie-talkies to talk.

The sun Did you know that the sun is a big, hot star? It gives us light and heat. The Earth orbits the sun every 365 days. Every living thing on Earth needs the sun to live.

The moon The moon orbits the Earth every 27.3 days. We can see the moon because of the light from the sun.

Stars We don't know how many stars there are in Space. Astronauts think there are so many stars that we can't count them.

Mars Astronauts think they could find life on Mars. They think this because there is water on Mars and all animals and plants need water.

Asteroids Asteroids are space rocks. They can be very big or quite small. Asteroids orbit some planets or the sun. They sometimes fall to Earth but they don't often hit the ground.

1 Space is very noisy because astronauts use walkie-talkies. ☐

2 Plants, animals and humans need the sun's light and heat to live. ☐

3 We don't know the number of stars in Space. ☐

4 Astronauts want to look for life on Mars. ☐

5 Asteroids are all very big. ☐

3 Look at Activity 2 again. Say why the sentences are false.

4 Read the interview with the astronaut on the International Space Station and match the questions with the answers.

Life on the Space Station

1 What's a space walk like?

2 What can you see out of the window?

3 What are you doing on the station?

4 How long are you there for?

5 When will you get home?

6 Is it dangerous?

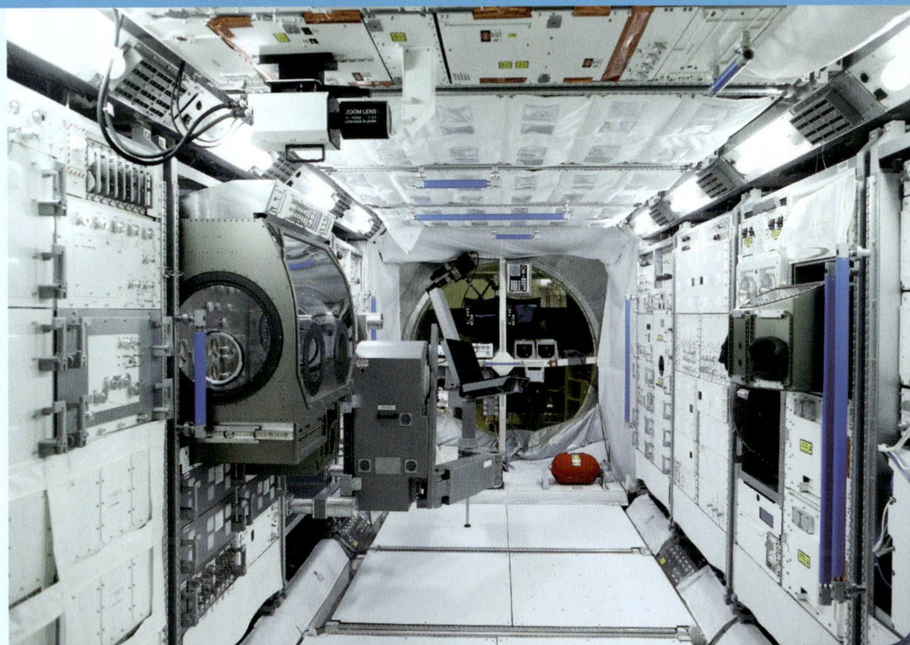

a Ten months. ☐

b I'll be home before my birthday in May. ☐

c I can see the deserts in Africa. ☐

d I'm learning about how plants grow in space. ☐

e Sometimes. You have to be careful when you do a space walk because things can hit you. ☐

f It's great. I get very excited when I do it. ☐

Super fact!

On Mars, there's a volcano that's three times bigger than Mount Everest!

5 Project Write three more questions to ask the astronaut, and draw a picture. In pairs, ask your questions and write your partner's answers.

Question: Is it difficult to put on your spacesuit?

Answer: Yes, it's difficult and very boring.

Talk and find out

Interview an alien

1 Choose a role card. Read and plan.

Student A

You are an astronaut. You are going to talk to an alien on the planet Og.

Think of questions to ask:

- his / her name and age
- what he / she does
- his / her family
- what Og is like
- other things which you want to know (How … ? Why … ?)

Ask and answer questions.

Student B

You are an alien who lives on the planet Og. You are going to talk to an astronaut from Earth. Think about:

- your name and age
- what you do
- your family
- what Og is like
- other things which you want to tell the astronaut

Ask and answer questions.

Useful language

Astronaut	Alien
Is this Og?	Yes, it is. Welcome to my planet!
What do you do … ?	I'm a …
Can you tell me about your family?	Yes, I've got …
What is Og like?	It's very …
How (do you travel on Og)?	We (have flying cars).
Why (have you got three heads)?	Because (we use …)

2 Act out your play.

A diary entry

1 Read the space diary entry. Number the pictures in order.

Friday, 12th March

Today we landed on the Moon. First we looked carefully out of the window. There were no monsters waiting for us. Then we put on our spacesuits. After that we opened the door of the spaceship. Finally we walked down the ladder to the moon.

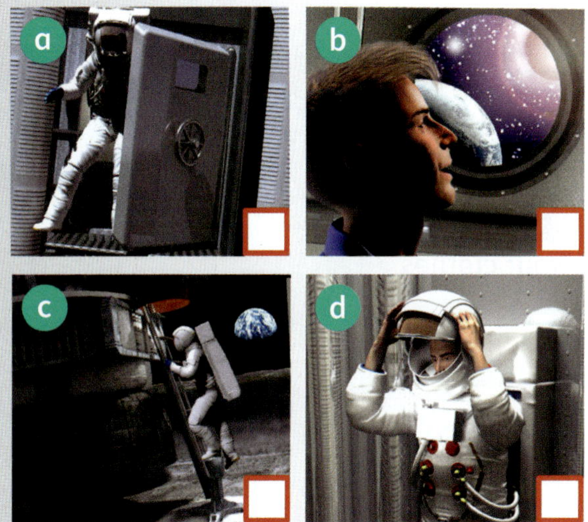

2 Complete this diary entry with the red words from Activity 1.

Wednesday, 7th June

Today we went on a long trip. (1) ________ we flew quickly from Planet XR3 into outer space. It was a fantastic journey and we saw a beautiful comet. (2) ________ we explored the centre of a very big galaxy called Galaxy 17.

We met with our friends from Jupiter there. (3) ________ we went round Galaxy 17. (4) ________ we returned home. Where will we go tomorrow?

3 Complete the notes about Thursday. Use your own ideas.

I saw: Jupiter and Mars

I flew to:

I explored:

I met:

Writing tip

Use words like *first*, *then*, *after that* and *finally* to show the order of events.

4 Write Thursday's diary entry. Use the red words from Activity 1.

9 At the campsite

1 111 **Listen and say the words. Then check with a friend.**

1 row a boat
2 sail a boat
3 dive into the water
4 dry your clothes
5 make a fire
6 make a raft
7 swing on a rope
8 put up a tent
9 collect wood

BIG QUESTION What do we know about camping?

2 112 **Listen and correct the sentences.**

1 Lucy wants to make a fire.
2 They are going to sail a boat.
3 Horax and Zelda are there.
4 Zelda is the Mysterious H.

3 **Play the guessing game.**

What was I doing at 5 o'clock?

Were you putting up a tent?

1 113 Look, read and number the sentences. Listen and check.

- a Let's get some cheese. ☐
- b There's some water in that glass. ☐
- c We must get some bread. ☐
- d There's a loaf of bread on the table. ☐
- e Let's get some lemonade. ☐
- f Can I have this can of lemonade, please? ☐
- g That's a big piece of cheese! ☐
- h Can you get three bottles of water, please? ☐
- i Open that packet of crisps carefully, please. ☐
- j Let's buy some crisps for the party. ☐

2 Complete using the words from the box. Say the phrases.

packet piece can loaf bottle

1. a ________ of tomatoes
2. a ________ of rice
3. a ________ of orange juice
4. a ________ of cake
5. a ________ of bread

3 114 Watch, listen and say.

Language focus

Give me **a bottle of** milk
And give me **a piece of** cheese.
Give me **a can of** tomatoes
And give me **some** lemonade, please.
Give me **a loaf of** bread
And give me **a packet of** rice.

4 Play the picnic game.

For the picnic I'm going to take a can of tomatoes.

For the picnic I'm going to take a can of tomatoes and a piece of cheese …

a bottle / can / loaf / packet / piece of and some

1 115 Listen and tick ☑ the activities you hear. Then sing the song.

This morning we put up our tent.
Then sailed on the sea.
We dived into the water
And now we're very hungry.

Pass me a loaf of bread,
A can of tomatoes too,
A bottle of milk, a piece of meat
And I'll make lunch for you.

This evening we collected wood
From a pile under a tree.
Then we made a great big fire
And now we're very hungry.

Pass me a packet of pasta,
A can of tuna too,
A bottle of sauce, a piece of cheese
And I'll make dinner for you.

2 What do you need for the perfect camping meal? Write a list.

A bottle of orange juice
A packet of crisps

3 Compare your list with a friend.

What's on your list?

A piece of …

1 117 Listen and complete the shopping list.

FOOD FOR OUR CAMPING TRIP

2 boxes of eggs

___ bottles of juice

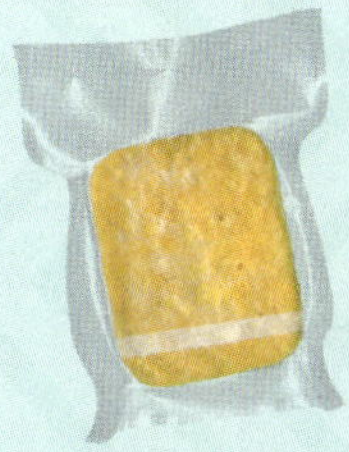

___ packets of cheese

___ loaves of bread

___ packets of crisps

___ bars of chocolate

___ packet of sweets

2 Complete with *many* or *much*. Say the sentences.

1 How bottles of orange juice do we need?

2 How cheese do we need?

3 How packets of crisps do we need?

4 How chocolate do we need?

3 118 Watch, listen and say.

Language focus

How many apples have we got?
We've got two.

How much water have we got?
Just one bottle.

4 Take it in turns to close your book. Play the memory game.

How much bread is there?

I think there are nine loaves.

The last line

1 119 How do Lucy and Ben know which way is west?

1

Lucy: We'd like to hire a rowing boat, please.
Assistant: How long do you want it for?
Ben: An hour, please.
Assistant: OK, that's £5.

2

Ben: Oh, where's the line? I'm getting very tired.
Lucy: Hey, look – on the oar! It's the last line!
Ben: You're right. 'There's the key to end this game'. Great, we've got all six lines!

3

Ben: OK, let's put the rhyme in order. I think this is the first line: 'In the lighthouse you will see'.
Lucy: And there's a lighthouse on the beach near the campsite! Come on!

4

Ben: Well, this is stair 33.
Lucy: And there's the picture.
Ben: I'm getting very excited.
Lucy: Me too.

5

Ben: Look, the key! Now we have to find the chest which this key opens.
Lucy: We have to climb more stairs first. I think we have to go to the top.

6

Ben: 'Climb more stairs and look out west.'
Lucy: Which way is that?
Ben: The sun sets in the west. It's over there.
Lucy: And look at the floor down here!

7

Lucy: That's it, Buster! Find the chest!
Ben: Here's the key. Look, it fits!
Lucy: Wow! This treasure is beautiful!
Ben: And now we can take it to the museum.

8

Horax: Why did I wear that ring? How stupid!
Zelda: No, it's the children who are stupid. They gave that treasure to the museum.
Horax: Again? Oh, no!

2 **Answer the questions.**

1 How long do Ben and Lucy hire a boat for? ______
2 Where do they find the last line? ______
3 Where is the lighthouse? ______
4 Where do they find the key? ______
5 What does Zelda think of the children? ______

Phonics

3 **Find a cup of tea in the story.**

4 120 **Listen and say.**

A piece of cake, a cup of tea. On the lake – just you and me.

1 Look at the pictures and match them with things on the list in the story below.

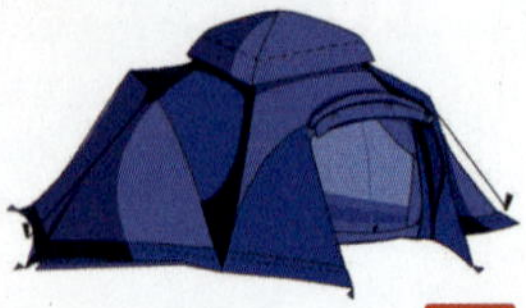 ☐ 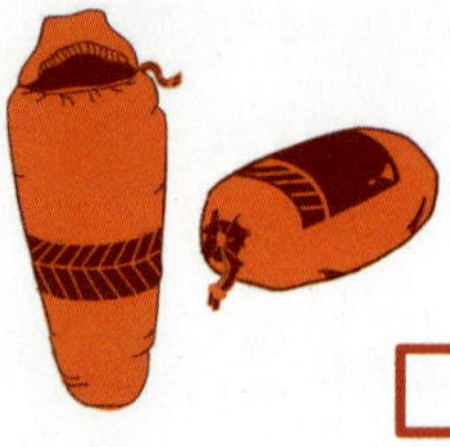 ☐  ☐  ☐  ☐

2 Read the story quickly and answer the questions.

1 Why does Mum buy flowers?

2 Where do the family go on the first day of their holidays?

3 What do the family forget to take to the campsite?

3 121 Read and listen. Check your answers.

Let's go camping!

'Let's go camping!' said Mum.
'Camping?' said Dad. 'What do we know about camping?'
'Well, everyone says it's fun,' said Mum.
'Hmm. I'm not so sure,' said Dad. 'I think I prefer hotels.'
But I liked the idea. 'Come on Dad,' I said. 'Let's do something different.'
'OK,' said Dad.
'Let's make a big list of all the things we need!' said Mum.
'A big list?' asked Dad. He looked a bit worried.
'Yes, we'll need a lot more than a tent,' Mum said.
And so we made a list. Mum wrote it and I added some notes.
'Flowers?' said Dad.
'Yes,' said Mum. 'To make our tent a home.'
We didn't have many of these things, so we spent the first day of our holidays in the camping shop.

- tent – with two rooms
- kettle
- sleeping bags – really warm ones
- food – chocolate, sweets and crisps
- mattresses – must be comfortable
- torch – a really cool one
- cooking stove
- plates, cups, knives and forks
- lots of warm clothes
- camping chairs
- flowers

'Wow, that is a lot of things!' said Dad. 'Are you sure you don't want a week in a hotel?' Dad asked.
'No,' Mum and I said. 'Camping's going to be fun.'
We took everything home and put it all on the kitchen table. There wasn't enough space, so we put some on the floor. An hour later, Mum came downstairs with two big suitcases of clothes. I made another big bag of food. I didn't want to forget the most important things!

Dad came in and looked at all the things on the floor. 'We're going to need a bigger car!' he said.

'Don't be silly,' said Mum. 'You take everything outside and I'll put it all in the car. I'm good at packing.'

Half an hour later Mum was finished. There was just enough space for three of us to sit in the car.

'Come on,' Dad said. 'Jump in. Let's go camping!'

Two hours later we arrived at the campsite. We parked the car under a tree.

'This looks like a good place for a tent,' Dad said. 'Let's get everything out of the car.'

Soon the bags from our kitchen floor were on the grass under the tree.

'OK,' said Dad. 'Who wants to help me put the tent up?'

'Which bag is the tent?' I asked.

'The big blue one,' Dad replied.

I looked everywhere. 'There is no big blue bag,' I said.

'Oh, no!' cried Mum. 'We left the tent at home!'

'Don't worry!' said Dad. 'There's a nice hotel just over there.'

4 Put the story in order.

- ☐ The family go shopping.
- ☐ The family put their camping things on the kitchen table.
- ☐ Mum wants to go camping.
- ☐ The family park under a tree.
- ☐ The family can't find the blue bag.
- ☐ Mum puts everything in the car.
- ☐ Mum writes a list.
- ☐ Dad points to a hotel.

5 122 Listen to a summary of the story. Write the four differences.

In the summary we have …

1 shoes instead of flowers.

2 ________ instead of ________.

3 ________ instead of ________.

4 ________ instead of ________.

6 Work with a friend.
What can the family do now?

Mum or Dad can drive back home and get the tent.

MEASUREMENTS

Watch and answer. How can we measure camping equipment?

1 (123) Listen and point.

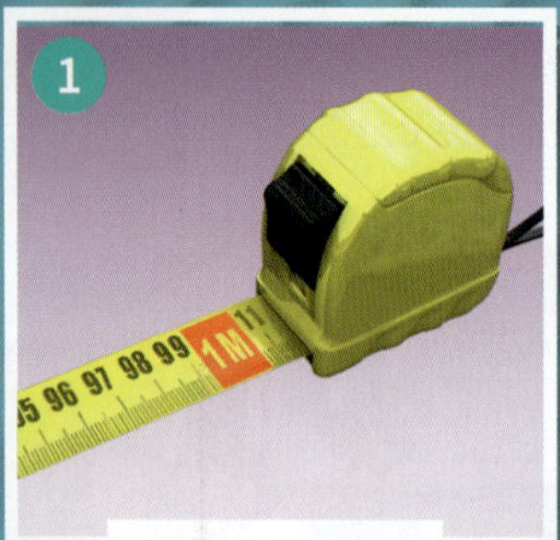

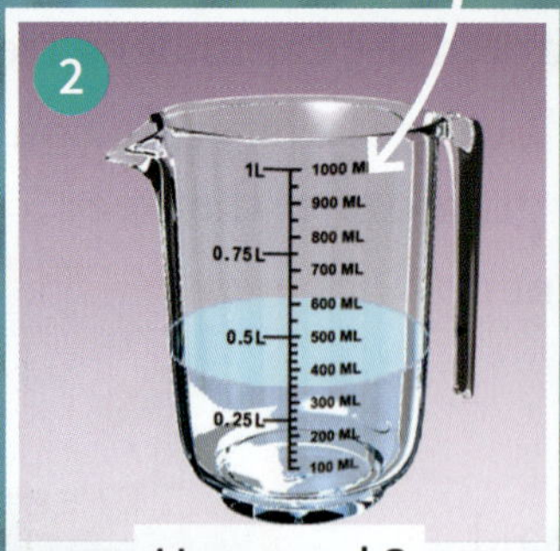

2 Read and write the questions next to the texts.

When we go camping, we sometimes need to know how many people can sleep in the tent, how heavy our backpack is or how much water we have. We can measure these things in different ways.

1 We can use a tape measure to find out how long, wide or high a tent is. We can measure it in centimetres (cm) and metres (m). We ask: *How long / wide / high is it?*

2 When we want to know how much water or soup we have, we can use a measuring jug. We can measure it in millilitres (ml) or litres (l). We ask: ______

3 We can use scales to find out how heavy a backpack is. We can measure it in grams (g) and kilograms (kg). We ask: ______

~~How long / wide / high is it?~~ How much water is there? How heavy is it?

3 (124) Match the measurements with the camping objects. Then listen and check.

1 It's 25 cm wide and 40 cm high.
2 It's small. It's about 15 cm long.
3 It's more than 2 m long, 1 m high and 1 m wide.

a a child's tent
b a backpack
c a torch

4 What can you measure in the classroom? Ask your partner.

How long is this pen?

Let's see. It's 10 cm long.

Super fact!

One of the biggest tents in the world is 150 metres high! It's in a country called Kazakhstan and it's got shops inside it and a river too.

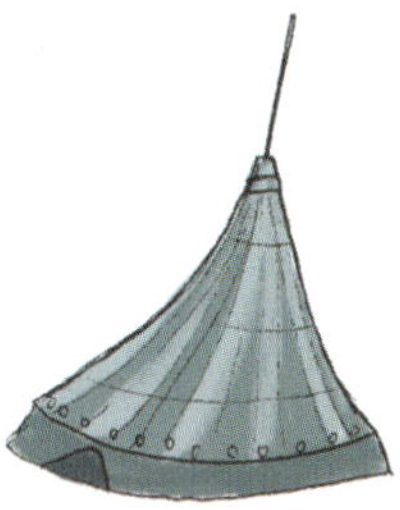

5 Look at these camping maths problems. What are the answers?

1

Jane's rope is 40 cm long and Beth's rope is 90 cm long. How much longer is Beth's rope?

2

Amir has got 75 ml of juice in his bottle and Noah has got 90 ml of juice in his bottle. How much more juice does Noah have?

3

Jane's can of fruit is 500 g and Amir's can of fruit is 900 g. How much heavier is Amir's can of fruit?

4

Noah's raft is 1 m and 50 cm wide and Beth's raft is 1 m wide. How much wider is Noah's raft?

6 Work with a partner. Write a camping problem for another pair to answer.

7 Project

Make an advertisement for something you would like to take on a camping holiday. What's it made of? What can you use it for? Write the measurements.

Talk and find out

Holiday plans

1 Make a class list of holiday plans on the board.

Go to the beach	Stay at home	Do a holiday club	Go abroad	Go camping
✓✓✓✓	✓✓✓✓✓	✓✓	✓	✓✓✓✓

2 Work in groups. Choose a holiday plan. Ask and answer. Make a poster.

What are you going to do on the beach?

I'm going to read lots of books.

3 Tell the class about your poster.

Four children are going to go to the beach. Bruno is going to learn to surf.

Paula is going to read lots of books on the beach.

Ana is going to fly her kite.

Lucía is going to eat lots of ice cream and build a big sandcastle.

A holiday leaflet

1 Read the leaflet. What do you like about this campsite?

Come to Clifftop Campsite!

Where is it?

This beautiful campsite is near the beach. You can come by train from Barrow (45 minutes) or by bus from Milton (5 minutes).

What can you do here?

You can learn to surf and sail a boat here because there is a water sports centre.

Where can you visit?

There's a lake near the campsite where you can see lots of different birds. The lighthouse in Clifftop is very old, so it's a fascinating place to visit.

2 Plan a leaflet for a campsite or holiday camp.

1. Fold a piece of paper for your leaflet.
2. Choose a real or imaginary place.
3. Find or draw pictures of the correct size.
4. Write texts in pencil on small pieces of paper.
5. Arrange your pictures and texts.

Clifftop Campsite

What has the campsite got?

We have got everything! This campsite has got shops and a café (with internet).

Prices:

Small tent
£30 (1 night)
£50 (weekend)
£120 (a week)

Big tent
£45 (1 night)
£75 (weekend)
£150 (a week)

3 Check your text.

1. Does your leaflet give useful information?
2. Are there any interesting adjectives?
3. Can you make longer sentences with:
   - *and*, *because*, *so* or *but*?
   - *who*, *which* or *where*?

4 Make your leaflet.

Writing tip

Use brackets (…) to include extra information.

Language focus Well done, Ben and Lucy!

Present simple questions

Do you **speak** English?	Yes, I **do**.	**Are** you happy?	Yes, I **am**.
Does John **like** pizza?	No, he **doesn't**.	**Is** it cold?	No, it **isn't**.
Do they **go** to your school?	Yes, they **do**.		

When **do** you **have** Maths?
How **does** he **spell** his name?
What**'s** your favourite number?
What time **do** you **have** lunch?

1 Complete the sentences.

1 _________ you tired?

2 _________ she like dogs?

3 What time _________ you get up?

4 _________ your English homework difficult?

Past simple questions

Did he **enjoy** the film?	No, he **didn't**.	When **did** he **see** it?	On Monday.
Were you at school on Friday?	Yes, I **was**.	**Was** it nice?	Yes, it **was**.

2 Put the words in order to make questions.

1 they / Did / win / match / the / ?

____

2 interesting / Was / lesson / the / ?

____

3 you / your / do / Did / homework / ?

____

4 Did / that / you / buy / jumper / where / ?

____

1 In the museum

Must / Mustn't

I **must go** to bed early tonight.
He **must be** more careful.
Dogs **must be** on a lead.
You **mustn't tell** anyone.
She **must be** there by 9 o'clock.
We **mustn't make** a noise.

1 Write *must* or *mustn't*.

1 I ________ tidy my room today.
2 They ________ do their homework tonight.
3 We ________ show this to anyone. It's a secret.
4 You ________ be quiet. Your little sister's sleeping.
5 We ________ talk in class. Our teacher gets angry.

Direct and indirect objects

I sang **my baby brother a song**.
Don't ask **them the same question**!
Don't tell **him the secret**!
Give **it a bath**, please.

2 Put the words in order to make sentences.

1 his / give / Rex / ball
____

2 show / your / me / picture
____

3 this / made / Dad / skateboard / me
____

4 take / some / flowers / Grandma / let's
____

5 stories / them / Grandpa / great / tells
____

2 The world around us

Past simple revision; connectors

They went to the park **and** they played football.
I was late **because** the bus didn't come.
He didn't study, **so** he didn't pass the test.
I went fishing, **but** I didn't catch anything.

1 Complete the sentences.

1 I didn't do my homework _________ I was very tired.
2 It wasn't a funny film, _________ I didn't laugh very much.
3 For my birthday I had a bike _________ we went to the zoo.
4 Mum loved sweets when she was little, _________ she didn't like chocolate.
5 It was rainy _________ it was windy too, _________ we didn't go for our picnic.
6 I was ill, _________ I didn't go to the party _________ I was in bed all day.

Could / Couldn't

I **couldn't speak** English when we first moved to the UK.
She **could play** the piano when she was three!
Could you **talk** when you were one? No, I **couldn't**.
Could they **dance** when they were younger? Yes, they **could**.

2 Write *could* or *couldn't*.

1 I _________ phone you because I was busy.
2 It was dark, so she _________ see anything.
3 We _________ speak Italian because we lived in Rome.
4 Dad _________ lift me up high when I was little. He can't now!
5 Mum _________ run very fast and she won all the school races.

3 Danger!

Past continuous

At two o'clock in the park …

I **was playing** with my friends.
Mum **was reading** a newspaper.
My friends **were running**.

You **were sleeping**.
We **were having** a lot of fun.
The cat **was eating** the picnic.

1 **Complete the sentences.**

1 I ________ playing the guitar.

2 My sister ________ watching TV.

3 The dog ________ chasing the cat.

4 Mum and Dad ________ working in the garden.

Past continuous questions

Yesterday evening …

What **were** you **doing**?	I **was helping** my dad.		
What **was** he **doing**?	He **was doing** the washing up.		
Was Mum **working**?	No, she **wasn't**.	**Were** you **reading**?	Yes, I **was**.
Were they **having** fun?	Yes, they **were**.	**Was** it **raining**?	Yes, it **was**.

2 **Complete the sentences.**

Think about yesterday afternoon.

1 ________ you watching TV? Yes, I ________.

2 ________ Dad playing the piano? No, he ________.

3 ________ your brothers swimming? Yes, they ________.

4 What ________ Mum doing? She ________ reading.

5 What ________ you doing? I told you! I ________ watching TV!

4 Two return tickets

at / in / on

School starts **at** nine o'clock.
My sister's birthday is **in** January.
Mrs York came to this school **in** 2011.
I can't sleep **at** night when it's very hot.
It's very hot **in** summer.
What was he doing **in** the morning?
I have swimming lessons **at** four o'clock **on** Wednesday afternoons.

1 Complete the sentences.

1 Mum met Dad _________ 1995.
2 The film starts _________ seven o'clock.
3 We went shopping _________ the afternoon.
4 I don't like playing outside _________ winter.
5 We're going to fly to Canada _________ Monday.

Past continuous and past simple

When the phone **rang**, I **was brushing** my teeth.
They **were playing** football when the storm **started**.
The cat **was chasing** a mouse when it **hit** its head.

2 Read and circle the correct words.

1 I **waited** / **was waiting** for Mum when I **saw** / **was seeing** the accident.
2 When it **started** / **was starting** to rain, we **walked** / **were walking** home.
3 He **played** / **was playing** the piano when his friends **arrived** / **were arriving**.
4 When I **tidied** / **was tidying** my room, I **found** / **was finding** some money.

5 Police!

Used to

They **used to live** near us. That cat **used to sleep** in its basket!

1 Put the words in order to make sentences.

1 cream / Mum / love / used / ice / to

____

2 used / hamsters / have / We / to / two

____

3 sister / long / used / My / have / hair / to

____

4 parents / live / My / used / in / to / America

____

5 be / Grandpa / to / a / officer / used / police

____

Had to

My dad **had to go** to school on Saturdays. The cat **had to sleep** in its basket last night.

2 Complete the sentences. Use *had to* and the words from the box.

tidy do run get up

1 We ______________ very early for the plane.

2 I ______________ my room at the weekend.

3 They ______________ fast to catch the bus.

4 He ______________ a lot of homework yesterday.

6 Mythical beasts

Comparatives and superlatives

My bike's **faster than** your bike.	It's **the fastest** train in the world.
Paul is **better** at Maths **than** me.	My dad's **the best** driver in the world.
We were **worse than** the other team.	It was **the worst** day of my life.
Music is **more interesting than** Art.	History is **the most interesting** subject.
Why is my school bag **heavier** today?	It's **the fattest** cat in town!

1 Complete the sentences.

1 His dad's car is ________ ________ than my dad's car. (expensive)

2 I'm ________ ________ you at Science. (bad)

3 Dan is ________ ________ boy in our class. (silly)

4 You're ________ ________ mum in the world. (good)

5 I'm two days ________ ________ my best friend. (old)

6 It's ________ ________ ________ computer game in the world! (exciting)

It looks like ...

What **do** zebras **look like**?	They **look like** black and white horses.
What **does** your sister **look like**?	She's got long brown hair and blue eyes.
What **does** your cat **look like**?	It usually **looks like** it's hungry!

2 Put the words in order to make questions.

1 do / like / look / What / pandas / ?

____

2 the / What / like / Phoenix / look / does / ?

____

3 does / friend / best / like / look / your / What / ?

____

7 Orchestra practice

Possessive pronouns

It's **my** bag. = It's **mine**.	It's **your** bag. = It's **yours**.
It's **his** bag. = It's **his**.	It's **her** bag. = It's **hers**.
It's **our** bag. = It's **ours**.	It's **their** bag. = It's **theirs**.

1 Complete the sentences.

1 Tim and Fred, is this your dog? No, it isn't ________.

2 Is this my hat? Yes, Grandpa. That's ________.

3 Is this Sue's coat? Yes, it's ________.

4 Is this your cat, Mike? Yes, it's ________.

5 Is this George and Henry's house?
No, ________ is the big house over there.

who / which / where

Dan's the boy **who** plays the guitar.
The pen **which** I lost is blue.
The house **where** Tabby lives has got a small garden.

2 Complete the sentences.

1 Gina is the girl ________ sits next to me.

2 The town ________ we live is near the sea.

3 The skateboard ________ I want costs £40.

4 Is he the boy ________ plays the trumpet?

5 Where's the cake ________ Grandma made?

6 This is the hall ________ we practise.

8 In the planetarium

Will

You**'ll** (You **will**) **be** famous one day.	They**'ll** (They **will**) **visit** the moon.
What **will** you **be** when you grow up?	I**'ll** (I **will**) **be** an astronaut.
Will it **be** difficult?	Don't worry. It**'ll** (It **will**) **be** easy.

1 Rewrite the sentences with *'ll*.

1 I will be a teacher.

____

2 They will be very happy.

____

3 It will rain next week.

____

4 He will be an actor.

____

5 We will visit other planets.

____

Adverbs

He shouted **angrily**. Our class did the test **badly**.
The alien spoke very **slowly**. The cat sang **loudly** all night.

2 Write adverbs to complete the sentences.

1 Please come ____________. (quick)

2 She paints ____________. (beautiful)

3 The baby smiled ____________. (happy)

4 Our teacher talks very ____________. (quiet)

5 That UFO's flying ____________. (dangerous)

9 At the campsite

a bottle / can / loaf / packet / piece of and some

a bottle of milk

a packet of biscuits

two loaves of bread

a loaf of bread

a can of lemonade

a piece of cake

Can I have **some** milk?

1 **Complete the sentences.**

1 a ________ of cheese

2 a ________ of crisps

3 a ________ of apple juice

4 a ________ of pears

How much / How many?

How much water do we need?
How much bread do we need?
How much milk do we need?

How many bottles of water do we need?
How many loaves of bread do we need?
How many eggs do we need?

2 **Complete the questions.**

1 How ________ carrots do we need?
2 How ________ cheese do we need?
3 How ________ packets of crisps do we need?
4 How ________ bottles of juice do we need?
5 How ________ oranges do we need?